DEVELOPING COUNTRIES AND WORLD TRADE

Performance and Prospects

DEVELOPING COUNTRIES AND WORLD TRADE

Performance and Prospects

Edited by Yılmaz Akyüz

UNCTAD
Geneva

TWN

Third World Network
Penang, Malaysia

Zed Books
London & New York

Developing Countries and World Trade:
Performance and Prospects
is published for and on behalf of the United Nations

UNCTAD
United Nations Conference on Trade and Development
Palais des Nations
CH-1211 Geneva 10, Switzerland

Third World Network
121-S Jalan Utama
10450 Penang, Malaysia

Zed Books Ltd,
7 Cynthia Street,
London N1 9JF, UK
and Room 400, 175 Fifth Avenue,
New York, NY 10010, USA

Distributed exclusively in the United States on behalf of Zed Books by
Palgrave
a division of St Martin's Press, LLC
175 Fifth Avenue,
New York, NY 10010, USA.

Printed by Jutaprint
2 Solok Sungei Pinang 3, Sg. Pinang,
11600 Penang, Malaysia.

ISBN   1 84277 410 7 hb (Zed Books)
ISBN   1 84277 411 5 pb (Zed Books)
ISBN   983 9747 93 2 (TWN)

A catalogue record for this book is available from the British Library.
US CIP is available from the Library of Congress.

NOTES

This book is based on the *Trade and Development Report (TDR), 2002*, Part Two. The research was guided and coordinated by Yılmaz Akyüz who also edited the final report. Empirical research for chapter 1 was carried out by Jörg Mayer, Ali Kadri and Arunas Butckevicius, with contributions from Richard Kozul-Wright and Juan Pizarro. Jörg Mayer was also responsible for much of the work in chapter 2. Research for chapter 3 was carried out by Mehdi Shafaeddin and Yuefen Li with contribution from Xiaobing Tang. Comments and suggestions were received from many people including Bob Rowthorn, Andrew Cornford, Detlef Kotte, Cape Kasahara, Heiner Flassbeck, Stefano Chiarlone, Amjad Singh, Yu Yongding, and Michael Mortimore; however, they are not responsible for any remaining errors or omissions.

Contents

Chapter 3
CHINA'S ACCESSION TO WTO: MANAGING INTEGRATION AND INDUSTRIALIZATION

List of tables

List of charts

List of boxes

Abbreviations

ACP	African, Caribbean and Pacific (group of countries)
AFTA	ASEAN Free Trade Area
ASEAN	Association of South-East Asian Nations
ATC	Agreement on Textiles and Clothing (of WTO)
BLS	Bureau of Labor Statistics (of the United States)
CARICOM	Caribbean Community
COMESA	Common Market for Eastern and Southern Africa
ECE	Economic Commission for Europe
ECLAC	Economic Commission for Latin America and the Caribbean
EEC	European Economic Community
EU	European Union
FDI	foreign direct investment
FFE	foreign-funded enterprise
GATT	General Agreement on Tariffs and Trade
GDP	gross domestic product
GSP	Generalized System of Preferences
GTAP	Global Trade Analysis Project
IMF	International Monetary Fund
ISIC	International Standard Industrial Classification
LDC	least developed country
MERCOSUR	Southern Common Market
MFA	Multi-Fibre Arrangement
MFN	most favoured nation
MOFTEC	Ministry of Foreign Trade and Economic Cooperation (People's Republic of China)
NAFTA	North American Free Trade Agreement (or Area)
NBTT	net barter terms of trade
NGLs	natural gas liquids
NIE	newly industrializing economy
NTM	non-tariff measure
OECD	Organisation for Economic Co-operation and Development
OPT	outward processing trade
PC	personal computer
PTA	preferential trade agreement
R&D	research and development
RCA	revealed comparative advantage
SCM	subsidies and countervailing measures (Uruguay Round Agreement on Subsidies and Countervailing Measures)

SITC	Standard International Trade Classification
SME	small and medium-sized enterprise
SOE	State-owned enterprise
TFP	total factor productivity
TNC	transnational corporation
TRAINS	Trade Analysis and Information System
TRIMs	Trade-related Investment Measures (WTO Agreement)
TRIPS	Trade-related Aspects of Intellectual Property Rights (WTO Agreement)
TRQ	tariff rate quota
UNCTAD	United Nations Conference on Trade and Development
UN/DESA	United Nations Department of Economic and Social Affairs
UNESCO	United Nations Educational, Scientific and Cultural Organization
UNIDO	United Nations Industrial Development Organization
USITC	United States International Trade Commission
VER	voluntary export restraint
WTO	World Trade Organization

Preface

It is a sign of troubled times when, in the search for solutions to the most pressing policy challenges of the day, it is considered necessary to look to earlier generations for guidance: a Marshall Plan – this time to fight global poverty – a Tobin tax to check financial volatility and a Keynesian spending package to combat deflationary dangers spring readily to mind. The source of the trouble is the gap between the rhetoric and the reality of a liberal international economic order. Nowhere is this gap more evident than in the international trading system. Even as Governments extol the virtues of free trade, they are only too willing to intervene to protect their domestic constituencies that feel threatened by the cold winds of international competition. Such remnants of neo-mercantilist thinking have done much to unbalance the bargain struck during the Uruguay Round.

Since the third session of the WTO Ministerial Conference, held in Seattle, a renewed effort has been made to address the concerns of developing countries, culminating in a different kind of bargain being struck at Doha. Developing countries, by agreeing to a comprehensive programme of work and negotiations, demonstrated their commitment to tackling global political and economic threats; in return, they expect that development concerns will be central to the negotiations. The challenge is now to translate an expanded negotiating agenda into a genuine development agenda.

One voice from the past stands out in the search for a more balanced trading system. In his statement to the first United Nations Conference on Trade and Development in March 1964, Raúl Prebisch, its then Secretary-General, called on the industrial countries not to underestimate the basic challenge facing developing countries in the existing system:

> *We believe that developing countries must not be forced to develop inwardly – which will happen if they are not helped to develop outwardly through an appropriate international policy. We also deem it undesirable to accept recommendations which tend to lower mass consumption in order to increase capitalization, either because of the lack of adequate foreign resources or because such resources are lost owing to adverse terms of trade.*

Prebisch understood that recommending "the free play of market forces" between unequal trading partners would only punish poorer commodity exporters at the same time as it brought advantages to the rich industrial core. His agenda to attack the persistent trade imbalance and create the essential external conditions for accelerating the rate of growth included new modalities of participation for developing countries in the trading system which would guarantee price stabilization and improved market access for primary exports, allow greater policy space to develop local industries and reduce barriers to their exports, establish more appropriate terms of accession to the multilateral system and reduce the burden of debt servicing. Although the participation of developing countries in the trading system has since gone through important changes, the minimum agenda put forward by Prebisch remains the basis for rebalancing that system in support of development.

Developing countries in world trade

Fundamentally, the basic policy challenge facing most developing countries remains how best to channel the elemental forces of trade and industry to wealth creation and the satisfaction of human wants. Shifting away from their dependence on the export of primary commodities towards greater production and exports of industrial products has often been viewed as a means of their participating more effectively in the international division of labour. Manufactures are expected to offer better prospects for export earnings not only because they allow for a more rapid productivity growth and expansion of production, but also because they hold out the promise of greater price stability even as volumes expand, thereby avoiding the declining terms of trade that have frustrated the long-term growth performance of many commodity-dependent economies.

Since the early 1980s, moves to rapidly liberalize trade and FDI have strongly influenced policy makers in many developing countries in their thinking about this challenge. Openness to international market forces and competition was expected to allow those countries to alter both the pace and the pattern of their participation in international trade, thereby overcoming balance-of-payments problems and accelerating growth, to catch up with industrial countries.

During this period, the exports of developing countries have, indeed, grown faster than the world average and now account for almost one third of world merchandise trade. Much of that growth has been in manufactures, which today account for 70 per cent of developing country exports; for some products developing country exports account for around half or more of world exports. More importantly, many developing countries appear to have succeeded in moving into technology-intensive manufactured exports, which have been among the most rapidly growing products in world trade over the past two decades, notably electronic and electrical goods.

However, on closer examination, the picture is much more nuanced. With the exception of a few East Asian first-tier newly industrializing economies (NIEs) with a significant industrial base, which were already closely integrated into the global trading system, developing country exports are still concentrated on products derived essentially from the exploitation of natural resources and the use of unskilled labour which have limited prospects for productivity growth and lack dynamism in world markets. Statistics showing a considerable expansion of technology-intensive, supply-dynamic, high-value-added exports from developing countries are misleading. Such products indeed appear to be exported by developing countries, but in reality those countries are often involved in the low-skill, assembly stages of international production chains organized by transnational corporations (TNCs). Most of the technology and skills are embodied in imported parts and components, and much of the value added accrues to producers in more advanced countries where these parts and components are produced, and to the TNCs which organize such production networks.

Indeed, while the share of developing countries in world manufacturing exports, including those of rapidly growing high-tech products, has been expanding rapidly, the income earned from such activities by these countries does not appear to share in this dynamism. On this score, a comparison between the developed and developing countries over the past two decades raises some initial worries. Although developed countries now have a lower share in world manufacturing exports, they have actually increased their share in world manufacturing value added over this period. Developing countries, by contrast, have achieved a steeply rising ratio of manufactured exports to gross domestic product (GDP), but without a significant upward trend in the ratio of manufacturing value added to GDP. Accordingly, the increase in the shares of developing countries in world manufacturing exports has not been accompanied by concomitant increases in their shares in world manufacturing value added, and in several countries the two ratios have tended to move in opposite directions. Certainly, few of the countries which pursued rapid liberalization of trade and investment and experienced a rapid growth in manufacturing exports over the past two decades achieved a significant increase in their shares in world manufacturing income.

Clearly, for many developing countries, getting the most out of the international trading system is no longer just a matter of shifting away from commodity exports. At the same time, many of the same forces that adversely affected price and productivity dynamics in the primary sector, including the competitive structure of markets, income elasticities and technological weaknesses, need to be re-examined in the light of recent trends associated with the increased participation of developing countries in the international trading system.

Dynamic products in world trade

Over the past two decades the value of world merchandise exports has grown at an average rate of around 8 per cent per annum, compared to less than 6 per cent growth in global output and income (in current dollars). Among the 225 products examined in this study, exports of some have grown at rates three times as fast as the growth in global income, whereas for others export values have declined in absolute terms. It is mainly primary commodities, but also some manufactures, that have registered sluggish or negative growth rates. The growth of trade in about one third of all products, including both primary commodities and manufactures, has lagged behind the growth of global income.

While manufactures generally constitute the fastest-growing products in world trade, there are also some agricultural products in this group, such as non-alcoholic beverages and cereals. Many of the fastest-growing manufactures in world trade, such as electronic and electrical goods, which now account for around one sixth of world exports, tend to be technology-intensive, often with a high research and development (R&D) content. A common feature of these market-dynamic manufactures is that the sectors in which they are produced exhibit strong productivity growth. This is less so for other market-dynamic products, such as textiles and clothing, and transport equipment, which have low- or medium-skill contents.

Differences in income elasticities, product innovation and changing consumption patterns, and shifts in competitiveness of industries across countries, can explain why some products are more dynamic in world markets than others. However, differences in the speed of liberalization of markets have also played a significant role. A particularly important influence in recent years has been the commercial policies of many developed countries, which limit access to their markets. Trade liberalization has been limited and slow in textiles and clothing along with other labour-intensive manufactures, compared to the pace of liberalization in other sectors. High tariffs and tariff escalation have been compounded by other overt forms of protection such as tariff rate quotas, as well as by the adverse impact of anti-dumping actions and product standards. The growing number of non-tariff barriers, especially against unsophisticated manufactures, has reinforced the prevailing patterns of market access, which favour high-tech products over low- and middle-range products that tend to gain importance in the early stages of industrialization.

Perhaps a more decisive influence on product dynamism has been the strategy of TNCs. The three product groups with the fastest growth rates over the past two decades, namely components and parts for electrical and electronic goods, labour-intensive products such as clothing, and goods with a high R&D content, have been most affected by the globalization of production processes through international production-sharing arrangements. The increased mobility of capital, together with continued restrictions over labour movements, has extended the reach of international production networks, thereby accelerating the growth of trade in a number of sectors where production chains can be split up and located in different countries. Favourable tariff provisions, often through regional arrangements, and fiscal and other incentives have encouraged this process, promoting a new pattern of trade whereby goods are processed in several locations before reaching final consumers, and the total value of trade recorded in such products exceeds their value added by a considerable margin. Trade based on specialization within such networks is estimated to account for up to 30 per cent of world exports.

Trade and industry: new linkages, old challenges

While developing countries as a whole appear to have become more active and dynamic participants in world trade over the past two decades, closer examination shows a great deal of diversity in the modalities of their participation in the international division of labour:

- First, many countries have not been able to move away from primary commodities, the markets for which are relatively stagnant or declining. However, growth in trade in several primary commodities has been as rapid as in some manufactures, and countries which have successfully entered such sectors have experienced a significant expansion in their exports and incomes;

- Second, most developing countries that have been able to shift from primary commodities to manufactures have done so by focusing on resource-based, labour-intensive products, which generally lack dynamism in world markets;

- Third, a number of developing countries have seen their exports rise rapidly in skill- and technology-intensive products which have enjoyed a rapid expansion in world trade in the past two decades. However, with some notable exceptions, the involvement of developing countries in such products is confined to labour-intensive, assembly-type processes with little value added. Consequently, the share of some of these countries in world manufacturing income actually fell. For others, increases in manufacturing value added lagged considerably behind their recorded shares in world manufacturing trade;

- Finally, a few countries have seen sharp increases in their shares in world manufacturing value added which matched or exceeded increases in their shares in world manufacturing trade. This group includes some East Asian NIEs which had already achieved considerable progress in industrialization before the recent shift to export drive in the developing world. None of the countries which have rapidly liberalized trade and investment in the past two decades is in this group.

Thus, most developing countries are still exporting resource- and labour-intensive products, effectively relying on their supplies of cheap, low-skilled, labour to compete. With the exception of the last group, they do not appear to have been able to establish a dynamic nexus between exports and income growth that would allow them to rapidly close the income gap with industrial countries. Although they as a whole appear to have become major players in world markets for dynamic products, they still account for only 10 per cent of world exports of products which score high in R&D content, technological complexity and/or economies of scale.

Making sense of a system in which many developing countries are vigorously expanding their foreign trade but are not rewarded by a comparable rise in income requires some hard thinking. A first step is to break with a casual style of empiricism, which takes the classification of manufactured traded goods at face value. Generally, developing countries participating in high-technology sectors are not involved in the skill- and technology-intensive parts of the overall production process. Consequently, their contribution to value added is determined by the cost of the least scarce and weakest factor, namely unskilled labour, whereas the rewards to scarce but internationally mobile factors such as capital, management and know-how are reaped by their foreign owners. It is thus the labour itself, rather than the product of labour, that is exported. Indeed, even in countries such as China and Malaysia, which have been highly successful in raising their shares in world manufacturing exports and value added through participation in international production chains, an important part of domestic value added is captured by profits earned on FDI.

Clearly, participation in the labour-intensive segments of international production networks can yield considerable benefits for countries in the early stages of industrialization and with a great deal of surplus labour. It can enable them to increase employment and per capita income even when value added generated is low. Furthermore, increased employment of low-skilled labour in activities linked to international production networks – whether organized by large TNCs producing a standardized set of goods in several locations, or through groups of smaller enterprises located in different countries and linked through international subcontracting – has certainly widened the possible range of sectors where industrialization can begin and the basic techniques and organizational skills, which are prerequisites for a more broad-based growth, can be acquired. However, that does not constitute a leap into a new pattern of rapid and sustained industrial growth.

These networks allow TNCs a good deal more flexibility in, and control over, their choice of investment locations. Moreover, their productive assets, such as know-how, design and technology, can be locked more tightly inside the firm thanks to barriers of entry that result from the high costs of managing and coordinating such complex units. The packaged nature of FDI can, in these circumstances, be the cause of a highly skewed distribution of the gains from trade and investment unless local bargaining power can bring a more balanced outcome, as it did for the first-tier East Asian economies. However, replicating the success of those countries is all the more difficult where such investment is highly mobile: locational advantages are easily won and lost through small cost changes or the emergence of alternative sites, giving rise to the danger of enclave economies where there is a persistently high dependence on imported inputs such as capital and intermediate goods. These problems can be particularly serious for middle-income countries which have been successful in early stages of industrialization but which now need rapid upgrading and productivity growth in order to advance further along the development path.

Competition and the fallacy of composition

What a country can earn from its participation in the trading system, including through value chains, depends, *inter alia*, on the global supply of the goods produced and exported relative to demand. Unfavourable trends on both counts, resulting in declining terms of trade for commodities, have been a longstanding source of anxiety for policy makers in developing countries. Relying on manufactured exports to galvanize growth was regarded as a solution to this problem.

As a result of increased participation of several highly populated, low-income countries in world trade in recent years, as much as 70 per cent of the labour force employed in sectors participating in world trade is low-skilled. However, there is still a considerable amount of surplus labour in such countries, and many large countries are not yet fully integrated into the international trading system. Thus, a simultaneous export drive by developing countries in labour-intensive manufactures, or increased competition among them to attract FDI as locations for labour-intensive processes of otherwise high-tech activities organized in international production networks, could rekindle the fallacy of composition problem, upsetting the development aspirations of outward-oriented economies and creating serious systemic tensions in the trading system. The dangers of overproducing standardized mass products with a high import dependence are typified by the electronics sector, where developing country export prices appear to be more volatile and to have fallen more steeply after 1995 than the same products traded among developed countries.

There are also more general signs that the prices of manufactured exports from developing countries have been weakening vis-à-vis those of the industrial countries in recent years. It is true that those developing countries that have achieved an impressive export programme on the basis of a dynamic manufacturing sector, such as the Republic of Korea, have also enjoyed favourable terms of trade with other developing countries, especially those exporting simple manufactures. Coupled with the fact that prices for a number of important developing country manufactures also appear to be increasingly volatile, there are grounds for concern. The design of export-oriented policies accordingly needs to take into account the probability of oversupply in the markets for labour-intensive manufactured exports from developing countries.

Because of the significant barriers to entry in high-skill and technology product lines associated with their high R&D contents and the high costs involved in organizing production chains, these markets are dominated by oligopolistic northern producers usually competing on the basis of quality, design, marketing, branding and product differentiation, rather than price. Final products that are less technology-intensive, such as machinery or transport equipment, which require the financing of very large and specific investments, are also among those with the highest concentration ratios of export market shares.

By contrast, the markets for labour-intensive goods have tended to be a good deal more competitive, especially in the past decade. These markets continue to provide opportunities for the new generation of industrializing economies. But weak growth and high unemployment in the advanced industrial economies have slowed the closure of their sunset industries. Moreover, most middle-income developing countries also persist in labour-intensive manufactures because their producers are finding it difficult to upgrade and diversify. Competitive pressures are further compounded by the way labour markets in developing countries accommodate the additional supply of labour-intensive goods through flexible wages, allowing firms to compete on the basis of price without undermining profitability. Competition among firms, including international firms, in developing countries becomes competition among labour located in different countries.

With a growing number of developing countries, including some with very large unskilled labour pools, turning to export-oriented strategies, it is the middle-income countries in Latin America and South-East Asia that appear most vulnerable to these dynamics. In particular, greater price competition in products of the electronics sector appears to have increasingly exposed traditional developing country exporters to the emergence of more competitive suppliers in countries with lower costs. In the absence of a rapid upgrading to high-skill manufactures needed to enable them to compete with more advanced industrial countries, these exporters may face a squeeze between the top and bottom ends of the markets for manufactures.

Implications of China's accession to the WTO

The accession of China to the WTO has raised the issue of the possible impact of the adoption of multilateral trade disciplines on the trade performance of China itself as well as of its trading partners. For China, it implies, above all, opening up its markets to greater foreign competition and commercial presence. The experience of liberalization episodes in Latin America and transition economies suggests that this can pose a challenge to economic policy makers. However, China's big advantage is that it is joining the multilateral system from a position of strength: spectacular success in export expansion; a sound and sustained balance-of-payments position; and abundant international reserves. Moreover, it is well placed to resist excessive import pressures linked to repressed consumer demand, which have derailed other liberalization episodes.

The most difficult challenges will be faced by enterprises and workers in the State-owned sector. These enterprises operate in agriculture, but are particularly prominent in heavy industry, including power, steel, chemicals and armaments, as well as the service sector. At the end of the 1990s they employed over 80 million people, and accounted for 38 per cent of GDP and about half of the country's total exports. Although reforms have been ongoing in this sector for well over a decade, many of the enterprises are in a weak financial position, operating at a sub-optimal level with outdated technologies and relying on high levels of protection. The terms of accession – notably removal of subsidies, reduction of tariffs and non-tariff measures, and elimination of preferential treatment – will exert considerable pressure on many of these enterprises, particularly as the competition will come mainly from firms in advanced countries. Considerable losses of jobs would seem unavoidable for both unskilled and skilled workers.

The consequences of restructuring and increasing unemployment in vulnerable sectors can be offset through industrial expansion elsewhere. Sectors such as clothing, electrical equipment, leather products and other light industries are expected to enjoy improved export opportunities following accession. The recent increase in inward FDI suggests that low labour and infrastructure costs remain a powerful attraction. However, it is unlikely that FDI will generate a large number of jobs; while exports from foreign-owned firms now account for more than 10 per cent of GDP, these firms employ less than 1 per cent of the total labour force. Even if employment in export industries dominated by these firms were to double, they cannot be expected to absorb more than a fraction of labour released elsewhere in the economy. Moreover, these firms are heavily dependent on imports, on top of which there is an outflow of profits, resulting in a net outflow of foreign exchange. Although an important part of total profits is reinvested, this contribution of foreign-funded enterprises to the balance of payments bears a certain resemblance to some countries in East Asia, such as Malaysia, before the outbreak of the financial crisis. If FDI simply serves to relocate labour-intensive processes to China, such an approach may create trade-offs and stiffer competition among countries with surplus labour and a high degree of reliance on FDI. Such an outcome can be avoided to the extent that FDI is used for technological upgrading and greater attention is paid to the role of domestic markets in absorbing surplus labour.

The growing presence of Chinese exporters is a matter of concern to many developing countries with a similar trading structure. Nevertheless, and despite low wages, China does not have an across-the-board cost advantage in manufacturing over other developing countries because of low productivity, particularly in the State-owned sectors. In labour-intensive manufacturing, including assembly operations in electronics, it is middle-income producers, such as the members of ASEAN and Mexico, that face the greatest exposure, particularly on third markets. These highly competitive markets are precisely the ones most vulnerable to the risk of fallacy of composition.

Concerns are heightened because the trading opportunities from further opening of the Chinese market are unlikely to favour its potential export competitors. China's imports are biased towards high-skill products and natural resources. Advanced industrial countries and the first-tier East Asia NIEs are likely to gain most, either because of an increased demand for imported parts and machinery linked to production networks or because of sizeable cost advantages over Chinese producers. However, liberalization of China's agricultural imports can be expected to present new export opportunities not only for some Asian countries, which already have high shares in China's imports of such products, but also for some Latin American and African countries.

China's challenge to integrate further into the world economy will require a full range of policies to smooth the adjustment process and maintain solid growth. It is important that it retain its autonomy and the option to use the exchange rate, if needed, to prevent serious disruptions to certain sectors of its economy. Because there is a limit to relying on labour-intensive exports, a rapid and well-sequenced technological upgrading in manufacturing that allows exports to shift to higher value-added and skill-intensive products will require a new strategy, designed to replace imported parts and components with domestic production while placing greater reliance on domestic markets for increasing productive employment. Properly managed, such a process could enable China to leapfrog the industrialization process instead of seeking to absorb the surplus labour in relatively low value-added, labour-intensive manufactures.

Policy issues

The basic policy issue facing developing countries in the trading system is not, fundamentally, one of more or less trade liberalization, but how best to extract from their participation in that system the elements that will promote economic development. For some this is still a matter of switching from primary commodities, but for many others it is a question of increasing the value-added component of manufacturing exports. The challenges facing China stand as a reminder that even the largest developing economies still require sufficient policy space to manage their integration into the global economy.

Since Seattle, concern has been expressed about the extent to which the multilateral trading rules may foreclose policy options that were part of the successful development strategies in the Asian NIEs as well as in many developed countries. Those concerns might have been eased if the increased market access expected from the Uruguay Round had been realized. Instead, a combination of continued barriers to market access, reduced policy space for nourishing competitive enterprises and promoting technological upgrading, along with excessive competition among developing countries in world markets for labour-intensive products and for FDI (in the labour-intensive segments of international production networks), has raised once again the risk of fallacy of composition.

At the fourth session of the WTO Ministerial Conference, held in Doha, the concerns of developing countries first raised in Seattle were acknowledged. The challenge now is to make the multilateral trading system more development-friendly. The outcome will be judged by the extent to which developing countries achieve greater market access without their policy options being restricted. The dynamics of the trading system underscore the urgency of making real progress in this respect.

It would be wrong to suggest that making good on the bargain struck in the Uruguay Round by providing improved access to markets in areas of interest to developing countries carries no, or only small, adjustment costs in industrial countries. Prolonged periods of high unemployment and slow growth in those countries have led many low-skilled communities to resist further concessions on trade. But renewed protectionism is not the way forward. Anxieties arising from increased competition can best be addressed by making sure that the full range of macroeconomic and structural policies is employed to accelerate growth and reduce unemployment. That is how developed countries absorbed the entry of low-cost producers in the 1950s and 1960s, and there is no reason to think that the design of a "win-win" package is beyond the technical competence of policy makers in the current era.

Developing countries also need to strike the right policy balance. Continuing efforts to ensure a pro-investment policy regime through an appropriate mix of macroeconomic and market pressures and incentives will be required to meet target growth rates of 6 per cent and above. But much more will be needed to stimulate dynamic export-investment linkages. Developing countries must be able to graduate across the full spectrum of manufacturing industries to ensure that more of the productive activities generating trade stay at home and to help avert the problems associated with fallacy of composition. This will call for a faster expansion of domestic markets and a rapid technological upgrading through targeted trade and industrial policies and a well-devised approach to FDI. The policies adopted by the East Asian NIEs for this purpose are well known. Success in upgrading, particularly by middle-income countries, will crucially depend on the extent to which obstacles to access to technology and industrial upgrading will be removed in the WTO review process.

Finally, many larger developing countries will need to find ways of utilizing domestic sources of growth more fully. This suggests that the outward orientation of their economies may decline as they grow richer and their home market expands. For smaller countries regional arrangements could provide the right context for galvanizing the forces of trade and industry. These played an important role in East Asia in facilitating the kind of staggered industrialization that is now required on a wider scale. Conventional economic thinking tends to dismiss these as second-best solutions for meeting development goals, and as a potential stumbling block on the road to a fully open and integrated multilateral system. However, these arguments are much less convincing when domestic firms still have weak technological and productive capacities and the global economic context is characterized by systemic biases and asymmetries.

Rubens Ricupero
Secretary-General of UNCTAD

Chapter 1

EXPORT DYNAMISM AND INDUSTRIALIZATION IN DEVELOPING COUNTRIES

A. Introduction

An important feature of world trade over the past three decades has been the growing participation of developing countries. Between 1970 and 1999 their merchandise exports grew at an average annual rate of 12 per cent, compared to 10 per cent for the world as a whole, resulting in their share in world merchandise trade increasing from less than one fourth to almost one third. During this period, developing countries also became important markets for each other's products: the share of trade among them reached 40 per cent of their total exports at the end of the last decade (chart 1.1). More importantly, these trends have been accompanied by a rapid transformation in the composition of their exports from primary commodities to manufactures, particularly since the early 1980s (chart 1.2). Manufactures accounted for 70 per cent of developing country exports at the end of the 1990s, after hovering at around 20 per cent during much of the 1970s and early 1980s, while the share of agricultural commodities fell from about 20 per cent to 10 per cent during the same period. Earnings from mineral and oil exports fluctuated considerably due to sharp changes in prices, but their overall trend was in a downward direction.

The belief that closer integration into the world trading system would create more favourable conditions for growth in developing countries and allow them to close the income gap with industrial countries has dominated commercial policy in most developing countries in recent years. Rapid liberalization of trade and foreign direct investment (FDI) has been the chosen policy approach, and in many cases this has indeed been accompanied by increased participation of developing countries in world trade, including a rapid expansion of their exports. However, as discussed in some detail in *TDR 1999*, for almost all developing countries imports expanded faster than exports, resulting in a deterioration of their trade balance. More importantly, their trade expansion has not necessarily been accompanied by faster growth in their gross domestic product (GDP) and by greater income convergence with industrial countries. The share of developed countries in world income (in current dollars) increased from less than 73 per cent in 1980 to 77 per cent in 1999, while that of developing countries stagnated at around 20 per cent. And although the share of developed countries in world manufactured exports fell from more than 80 per cent to about 70 per cent during this period, their share in world manufacturing income (value added) rose. Among the developing countries, it was mainly the East Asian economies that improved their share in world manufacturing income. Their success in combining expansion of trade with growth in income enabled them to continue to close the gap with richer industrial countries. Elsewhere, rapid liberalization has failed to increase exports of manufactures; or where growth in such exports has occurred, it has not been accompanied by concomitant increases in domestic manufacturing value added, but, rather, by rapid expansion in manufacturing imports. The gap between growth in manufacturing exports and income is also visible in most East Asian economies, except the major ones in the first-tier newly industrializing economies (NIEs).

Chart 1.1

SHARE OF TRADE AMONG DEVELOPING COUNTRIES IN THEIR TOTAL EXPORTS, BY MAJOR PRODUCT GROUP, 1975–1999

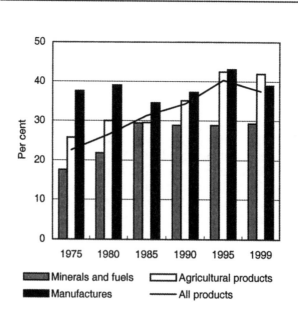

Source: *United Nations Monthly Bulletin of Statistics* database.

✦ *Chart 1.2*

**COMPOSITION OF MERCHANDISE EXPORTS FROM DEVELOPING
COUNTRIES, BY MAJOR PRODUCT GROUP, 1973–1999**

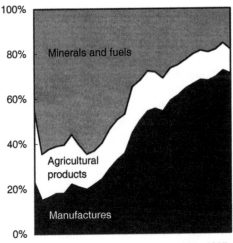

Source: See chart 1.1

These varying experiences suggest a complex relation between commercial policies and trade performance, and, more generally, between trade and growth, and they rule out an unequivocal causal link from the former to the latter.[1] Indeed, the relationship between trade, industrialization and growth depends, *inter alia*, on the pattern of integration and the location of countries in the international division of labour. Success in entering lines of production with significant potential for global demand expansion, high value added and rapid productivity growth widens the scope for the exploitation of increasing returns from

---

[1] Indeed, neither economic theory nor longer historical experience can confirm such an unequivocal causal link from trade to growth. While the mainstream literature has often focused on efficiency gains and welfare effects of improved resource allocation resulting from free trade, it has not been able to establish a strong causal link between trade and the two main sources of growth, namely capital accumulation and productivity growth. For controversies over the relationship between trade and development, see Srinivasan and Bhagwati (1999); and Rodrik (1999).

larger markets, and enhances the role of trade in economic growth. By contrast, concentrating on the export of goods with sluggish global demand and/or persistent excess supply endangers the growth process by leading to terms-of-trade losses and draining investible resources. Similarly, focusing on activities with limited potential for productivity growth can constrain growth once underutilized labour and natural resources are exhausted; productivity growth then becomes the single most important source of increase in per capita income. Thus, to the extent that it is feasible for a developing country to concentrate its production and exports on what can be called "dynamic" products with respect to their global demand potential (market-dynamic products) and productivity potential (supply-dynamic products), the country will be able to reduce the risk of its export markets becoming rapidly saturated as a result of more and more countries concentrating their export drives on the same sectors; it will also be able to exploit the potential for long-term productivity growth in the context of export expansion.

This chapter examines the evolution of world trade over the past two decades by focusing on various categories of products and the pattern of participation of developing countries in their production. In particular, it analyses the extent to which these countries have been successful in increasing their exports in market-dynamic, high value-added or supply-dynamic products. It is shown that while world trade has, on average, expanded faster than world income, due to the increased integration of markets, there are considerable differences in the rates of expansion of trade in different products. Generally, trade in skill- and technology-intensive manufactures has been increasing much faster than that in labour-intensive and resource-based manufactures and primary commodities, although certain products in the latter categories have also shown considerable dynamism. These differences cannot be explained in terms of differences in income elasticities or shifts in comparative advantage alone. Policies governing market access also appear to have played a major role, favouring skill- and technology-intensive sectors in which industrial countries have a competitive edge over agricultural commodities and middle-range manufactures, which are more important for less advanced countries. Another factor in the varying rates of expansion of trade in different products is the increased mobility of capital. This, together with continued restrictions on labour mobility, has extended the reach of international production networks in a number of products in which the production process can be partitioned into different segments that can be located in different countries according to their factor endowments and costs. Such arrangements have rapidly expanded trade in a number of products such as computers and office equipment; telecommunications, video and audio equipment and semiconductors; as well as clothing. They have also led to a greater involvement of developing countries in world trade in manufactured products. Policies in both developing and industrial countries have contributed to this process. Developing countries facilitated the operation of transnational corporations (TNCs) in their territories, while industrial countries facilitated market access for imports of goods containing inputs that originated in their own economies and were produced either in the foreign assembly plants of these TNCs or under contractual or outsourcing arrangements.

The evidence on the modalities of participation of developing countries demonstrates that with the exception of the first-tier NIEs – which had already become closely integrated with the global trading system and established a significant industrial base – the exports of developing countries are still concentrated on the exploitation of natural resources or unskilled labour; these products generally lack dynamism in world markets. Statistics showing a considerable expansion of technology- and skill-intensive exports from developing countries are misleading. Much of the skills in these exports are embodied in components produced in the technologically more advanced countries, while developing countries are engaged mainly in the low-skill, low-value-added assembly stages of global production chains generally organized by TNCs. Thus expansion of such exports has not been accompanied by concomitant increases in value added and income earned in developing countries. Much of the value added contained in these products still accrues to foreign owners of capital, know-how and management. While involvement in these activities may yield considerable benefits for countries at earlier stages of industrialization by allowing fuller utilization of their surplus labour, it may lead to problems relating to fallacy of composition when too many countries simultaneously attempt to enter these markets, a topic taken up in the next chapter. For the more advanced developing countries, where further progress in industrialization and development depends on rapid technological upgrading and productivity and wage growth, participation in the low-wage, labour-intensive segments of international production networks may not be an effective way to achieve their objectives.

Since markets do not automatically generate the incentives needed to alter the pace and pattern of integration into the global economy or overcome the impediments to a more dynamic interaction between trade and growth, there is a considerable role for policy. The evidence and the analysis presented here can thus help identify options available to policy makers in developing countries in their strategic approaches towards the integration of their economies into the international trading system, as well as the risks associated with misguided and excessive reliance on foreign markets and capital. Most developing countries will need to rapidly upgrade production to more market- and supply-dynamic products, instead of extending the existing patterns of production and trade. In most cases, upgrading of exports should involve replacing imported skill- and technology-intensive parts and components with domestically produced ones, thus raising the domestic value-added content of output and exports. Larger economies, heavily dependent on exports, may also need to increase their reliance on domestic markets in order to sustain growth and accelerate job creation, rather than concentrating on labour-intensive exports in the low-value-added segments of international production networks.

B.   Dynamic products in world trade

During the past two decades, the value of world merchandise exports has grown at an average rate of more than 8 per cent per annum. However, there have been considerable differences in the growth rates of trade in individual products. Among the 225 products covered by this analysis, some grew at rates twice as fast as the average growth in world trade, whereas for others export values declined in absolute terms, with declines exceeding 3 per cent per annum for some primary products (see annex A). Mainly primary commodities, but also some manufactures (notably machinery falling in the SITC 71 and 72 product divisions) registered sluggish or negative growth rates. Varying growth rates for different products have also meant considerable changes in the composition of international trade. These changes, however, have not occurred smoothly. There has been considerable year-to-year volatility in growth rates around the trend. Such variations have differed significantly for different products, with some showing greater stability and predictability over time than others.

Both longer-term trends and short-term variations in growth rates of exports show the combined effects of changes in prices and volumes. These are not unrelated; given the factors determining the aggregate world demand for a product, excessive supply to world markets tends to depress prices, resulting in stagnant or even declining export revenues. This phenomenon is known to be particularly important for primary commodities, since for most manufactures shortage of demand often, though not always, leads to a relatively quick adjustment in the volumes supplied rather than to a sharp drop in prices. This issue will be addressed in the next chapter in the context of fallacy of composition and terms of trade. Here the analysis of market dynamism of products is concerned with export earnings rather than export volumes, since, for most products, separate volume and price data are not available. However, readily available evidence suggests that the ranking of products would remain largely unchanged if growth rates of products in world exports could be calculated on the basis of constant rather than current prices (see annex B).

Table 1.1 shows the trend growth rates for the period 1980–1998 of the 20 most dynamic products in world trade.[2] Most of these products fall into four categories:

- electronic and electrical goods (SITC 75, 76, 77);
- textiles and labour-intensive products, particularly clothing (SITC 61, 65, 84);
- finished products from industries that require high R&D expenditures and are characterized by high technological complexity and/or economies of scale (SITC 5, 87); and
- primary commodities including silk, non-alcoholic beverages and cereals (SITC 261, 111, 048).

The fastest growing category of products, electronic and electrical goods, also accounts for a sizeable share in world exports; in this category, the three fastest growing product groups (transistors and semiconductors; computers; and parts of computers and office machines) alone increased their share in world exports almost four times, from 2.6 per cent in 1980 to 9.7 per cent in 1998. Taken together, the share in world exports of the seven groups of electronic and electrical products included in table 1.1 almost tripled to reach about 16 per cent in 1998. By contrast, the share in world exports of dynamic primary commodities is small, which suggests that their strong growth over the past two decades has been due, at least partly, to the fact that they started from a low base.

---

[2] In this chapter no formal distinction has been made between dynamic and non-dynamic products. The analysis uses an ordering of products according to their recorded growth rates in world trade since 1980 (see table 1.A1 in annex A). A formal distinction would require a threshold; the average growth rate of world income over the same period could provide an appropriate measure for this purpose.

Table 1.1

EXPORT VALUE GROWTH AND SHARE IN TOTAL EXPORTS[a]
OF THE 20 MOST MARKET-DYNAMIC PRODUCTS, 1980–1998

(Per cent)

SITC code	Product group	Average annual export value growth 1980–1998	Share in total world exports 1980	Share in total world exports 1998	Share in total exports from developing countries 1980	Share in total exports from developing countries 1998
776	Transistors and semiconductors	16.3	1.0	4.0	1.9	7.7
752	Computers	15.0	0.9	3.4	0.2	5.0
759	Parts of computers and office machines	14.6	0.7	2.3	0.3	3.6
871	Optical instruments	14.1	0.1	0.3	0.0	0.3
553	Perfumery and cosmetics	13.3	0.2	0.5	0.1	0.2
261	Silk	13.2	0.0	0.0	0.0	0.0
846	Knitted undergarments	13.1	0.3	0.6	0.8	1.4
893	Plastic articles	13.1	0.6	1.2	0.6	1.1
771	Electric power machinery	12.9	0.3	0.6	0.2	0.8
898	Musical instruments and records	12.6	0.3	0.7	0.2	0.5
612	Leather manufactures	12.4	0.1	0.1	0.1	0.2
111	Non-alcoholic beverages	12.2	0.1	0.1	0.1	0.1
872	Medical instruments	12.1	0.2	0.4	0.1	0.2
773	Electricity distribution equipment	12.0	0.4	0.7	0.3	1.0
764	Telecommunications equipment, and parts	11.9	1.5	3.0	1.7	2.9
844	Textile undergarments	11.9	0.2	0.3	0.8	0.8
048	Cereal preparations	11.9	0.2	0.4	0.1	0.2
655	Knitted fabrics	11.7	0.2	0.3	0.1	0.6
541	Pharmaceutical products	11.6	1.1	2.0	0.4	0.6
778	Electrical machinery	11.5	1.1	1.7	0.7	1.5
	20 most dynamic products	12.9	9.5	22.6	14.1	28.7
	Memo item:					
	World exports[b]	8.4				
	Developing country exports[b]	11.3	15.4	24.3		

Source: UNCTAD secretariat calculations, based on United Nations Department of Economic and Social Affairs (UN/DESA), *Commodity Trade Statistics* database.

Note: SITC code numbers refer to *Standard International Trade Classification, Revision 2*. For export value growth rates of other product groups, see annex 1.A.

 a Excluding fuels.

 b Total of all product groups listed in annex 1.A.

These fastest growing products have all shown yearly variations around their trend growth rates. Such variations reflect fluctuations and shifts in the determinants of trade in different products such as growth in global income, product innovation and policies affecting market access and integration, including international production networks (discussed in the next section). In general, the most market-dynamic manufactures, with high shares in world trade, show smaller variations around their trend values than less dynamic manufactures and primary commodities. Accordingly, for such products, current export values are better predicted by their past values than they are for less dynamic products. By contrast, the vast majority of those products for which export values are least predictable on the basis of their past behaviour also ranks low in terms of market dynamism.

However, all products have occasionally shown large deviations from their trend growth rates. Certain non-fuel primary commodities experienced their fastest rates of growth in export values in 1987 and 1988, years of rapid and synchronized expansion in the major industrialized countries; yet many others registered their lowest growth rates in 1997 and 1998, during the East Asian crisis. In both instances, sharp swings in commodity prices appear to have played a key role. Most of the dynamic manufactures also experienced their fastest rates of growth during the period 1986-1988, and their slowest growth rates during the 1980-1982 recession in the major industrialized countries. There is also evidence to suggest that a structural break occurred during the period 1986-1988 in the longer-term trends of export values of both non-fuel primary commodities and manufactures, possibly reflecting the shift in some major developing countries towards export-oriented strategies as well as the growing importance of international production networks, discussed below.[3]

The increased emphasis on exports by most developing countries appears to have been associated with a significant increase in the share of dynamic products in their export earnings during the past two decades (table 1.1). However, such products continue to account for a relatively small proportion of their total merchandise exports. The combined share of the three fastest growing electronic and electrical products in developing country exports in 1998 was only about 16 per cent, despite a sevenfold increase since 1980. And the share of all electronic and electrical products in developing country exports increased fourfold, from 5.3 per cent in 1980 to 22 per cent in 1998. Most developing countries which are considered to have been marginalized in the context of world trade, continue to rely on products that are subject to high volatility in the short term and show a declining trend in world trade over the longer term.

---

[3] The evidence is based on an analysis of one-step forecast errors and of a Chow test.

Although developing countries as a whole appear to have become major players in markets for many dynamic products, it is only in knitted undergarments that the share of developing countries in world exports exceeds that of developed countries. Developing countries account for only 10 per cent of world exports of products which score high in R&D content, technological complexity and/or economies of scale (table 1.2). In this category, only in optical instruments do they account for about 30 per cent of world exports. The share of developing countries in the total exports of parts and components for electrical and electronic goods is about 40 per cent, while for telecommunications equipment and parts of electric circuit equipment it is about a quarter of the total value. It should be noted that this refers to shares in gross export values, thus involving double counting of imported parts and components. As discussed in subsequent sections, the picture is even less promising in value-added terms, particularly where developing countries are involved in low-skill, low-value-added assembly stages of global production networks, as in electronics. The evidence discussed in annex B suggests that the export values of the most market-dynamic products from the electronics industry have been subject to a higher degree of volatility in developing countries than in the industrialized countries. Similarly, since the mid-1990s, the prices of these products seem to have fallen more steeply in developing countries than in developed countries.

C. Factors contributing to trade expansion in different products

Expansion of world trade is closely related to growth in world output and income. However, the link is neither linear nor uniform across all products. While world trade in non-fuel products grew (in current dollars) at an average rate of more than 8 per cent per annum over the past two decades, the growth rate of global output and income (in current dollars) was below 6 per cent. Moreover, trade in many products grew much faster than global output and income; for some products at the top of the list in table 1.1 and annex A, trend growth rates were almost three times the growth in world income and output. By contrast, growth of trade in a large number of products (71 out of the 225 products listed in annex A), including both primary commodities and manufactures, lagged behind growth of global income; indeed, as noted above, trade in some of these products shrunk in absolute terms.

Against this background, a number of questions arise: Why has total world trade in non-fuel products been growing faster than world output

Table 1.2

**SHARES OF MAIN EXPORTERS AND OF DEVELOPING ECONOMIES IN
WORLD EXPORTS OF THE MOST MARKET-DYNAMIC PRODUCTS,[a] 1998**

(Per cent)

Rank	SITC code	Product group	Share of developing countries	Main exporting countries (Share)	
1	776	Transistors and semiconductors	46	United States (17) Japan (15) Singapore (10)	Republic of Korea (10) Malaysia (7)
2	752	Computers	36	United States (13) Singapore (13)	Japan (10) Netherlands (9)
3	759	Parts of computers and office machines	38	United States (17) Japan (14) Singapore (9)	Taiwan Province of China (7) Malaysia (6)
4	871	Optical instruments	30	Japan (22) United States (17) Republic of Korea (12)	Germany (10) China (5) Hong Kong (China) (5)
5	553	Perfumery and cosmetics	10	France (28) United States (12)	United Kingdom (12) Germany (11)
6	261	Silk	87	China (70) Germany (9)	India (3)
7	846	Knitted undergarments	57	China (16) United States (8) Turkey (6)	Italy (6) Mexico (5)
8	893	Plastic articles	23	United States (14) Germany (13)	China (7) Italy (7)
9	771	Electric power machinery	37	United States (11) Germany (10)	China (9) Japan (9)
10	898	Musical instruments and records	18	United States (20) Japan (12) Ireland (12)	Germany (8) United Kingdom (7)
11	612	Leather manufactures	45	Italy (16) Taiwan Province of China (11) China (2)	United States (7) India (6) Republic of Korea (6)
12	111	Non-alcoholic beverages	22	France (19) Canada (7) United States (7)	Belgium/Luxembourg (7) China (7)
13	872	Medical instruments	12	United States (27) Germany (12) United Kingdom (7)	Japan (6) Ireland (6)
14	773	Electricity distribution equipment	34	Mexico (16) United States (14) Germany (9)	Japan (6) France (4)
15	764	Telecommunications equipment, and parts	24	United States (15) United Kingdom (9)	Japan (9) Sweden (7)
16	844	Textile undergarments	4	United States (30) United Kingdom (23) France (11)	Germany (9) Canada (5)
17	048	Cereal preparations	14	Italy (11) Germany (10)	France (10) United Kingdom (8)
18	655	Knitted fabrics	54	Taiwan Province of China (20) Republic of Korea (16) Germany (8)	Italy (8) China (8)
19	541	Pharmaceutical products	8	Germany (15) Switzerland (11)	United Kingdom (10) United States (10)
20	778	Electrical machinery	23	Japan (17) United States (13) Germany (13)	United Kingdom (7) Mexico (6)

Source: See table 1.1.
Note: See UNCTAD, *Handbook of Statistics* (table 4.4) for the main exporters of these products within the group of developing countries.
   a Product groups ranked by growth in export value, 1980–1998.

and income? Why has trade in some products been growing much faster than in others, and at rates several times the trend growth of world income? What is the significance of these trends for economic growth and development?

It has long been recognized that income is one of the principal factors that determines demand, and that there are significant differences among products with respect to their income elasticity. Differences in income elasticities can be expected to play an important role in disparities in the growth rates of broad product categories in world trade. For example, the relatively low income elasticity of demand for most agricultural products seems to have played a major role in the steady decline in the share of agriculture in developing country merchandise exports (chart 1.2). However, large differences in the ranking of individual products belonging to the same broad product categories according to their dynamism in export markets during the period 1980–1998 suggest that additional factors must have exerted a major influence on their performance in world trade. Although product-specific estimates of income elasticities are not available, it is unlikely that the ranking of products according to their performance in world trade would coincide with their ranking according to income elasticities. Indeed, policies governing market access and international production networks appear to have played a greater role in the differential growth of world trade in different products through their impact on the speed with which markets in various products are globally integrated.

1. Income growth and demand

The observation that growth of world trade in manufactures is faster than trade in primary products is not new. As incomes rise, a smaller share of household budgets tends to be spent on food, which implies that the share of food in world consumption and trade will tend to decline, unless relative production costs rise. For agricultural and industrial raw materials, demand grows less rapidly than income for several reasons: the shift in main consuming countries towards an economic structure based on products and services that require less raw material input, the development of synthetic substitutes (in particular for cotton, rubber and wool), and the general decline in the intensity of use of such raw materials in industrial production are some of the main reasons.

Income elasticity of demand also reflects the impact of product innovation on spending patterns. Such innovations can result in sharp increases in spending on certain product categories, once new products become accessible for mass consumers in the household sector and business. In this sense, the more innovative among manufacturers, often (though not always) enjoy more rapidly expanding markets for their products, thereby attaining faster growth. Over the past few years, economic growth in major developed countries, in particular the United States, has been closely linked to the increasing use of information technology products (including computer hardware and software, and telecommunications equipment) combined with rapidly improving technology for producing computers. Indeed, in the United States, the demand for information technology products, particularly new ones such as mobile telephones and personal computers, exceeded the pace of income growth by a considerable margin, resulting in an increase in the share of these products in income, from an average of 3.3 per cent during the period 1974–1990 to 6.3 per cent during the period 1996–1999 (Oliner and Sichel, 2000). This, together with the rapid development of sourcing from overseas sites (see below), appears to have played an important role in the rapid growth of world trade in such products.

Not only manufactures, but also primary products, differ in their market potential and contribution to export earnings. For example, there are several categories of unprocessed and processed foods that can be identified as high-value products and/or have income elasticities not only much higher than traditional agricultural products, but also in excess of unity.[4] The standards of quality, safety, packaging and delivery of such products are, in many respects, more typical of modern manufacturing than traditional agricultural products, including basic food commodities. In terms of market dynamism, this set of products has performed well compared to other agricultural primary commodities: export earnings of developing countries in several of these product categories now exceed their earnings from traditional primary commodities such as cereals, cocoa, tea or natural rubber. Moreover, the rapid expansion of such exports has contributed to growth in agricultural output and total food production in a number of developing countries, such as Brazil, China and Thailand, as well as to rapid GDP growth, for example, in Chile and Israel.

Seven of these food categories have been among the most market-dynamic agricultural products over the past two decades (table 1.3) with

---

[4] According to Jaffee and Gordon (1993) and World Bank (1994), these are: meat and meat products; dairy products; fish and fishery products; vegetables; fruits and nuts; spices; and vegetable oils.

Table 1.3

SHARES OF MAIN EXPORTERS AND OF DEVELOPING ECONOMIES IN WORLD EXPORTS OF THE MOST MARKET-DYNAMIC AGRICULTURAL COMMODITIES,[a] 1998

(Per cent)

Rank	Rank among all products	SITC code	Product group[b]	Share of developing countries	Main exporting countries (Share)	
1	6	261	Silk	87	China (70) Germany (9)	India (3)
2	12	111	Non-alcoholic beverages	22	France (19) Canada (7) United States (7)	Belgium/Luxembourg (7) China (7)
3	17	048	Cereal preparations	14	Italy (11) Germany (10)	France (10) United Kingdom (8)
4	23	098	Preserved food	17	United States (16) France (12) Germany (8)	China (5) Netherlands (6)
5	27	062	Sugar preparations	25	United Kingdom (10) Germany (9) Spain (9)	United States (7) Belgium/Luxembourg (6)
6	31	122	Manufactured tobacco	24	United States (29) Netherlands (16)	United Kingdom (10)
7	33	073	Chocolate	7	Germany (16) Belgium/Luxembourg (13) France (11)	United Kingdom (8) Netherlands (7)
8	67	036	**Fresh crustaceans**	70	Thailand (12) Indonesia (7) Canada (6)	India (6) Ecuador (6)
9	71	245	Fuel wood and charcoal	41	Latvia (15) Indonesia (10) China (10)	France (6) Poland (5)
10	72	034	**Fresh fish**	37	Norway (13) United States (7) Denmark (5)	China (5) Taiwan Prov. of China (5) Chile (5)
11	81	269	Waste of textile fabrics	16	United States (22) Germany (15)	United Kingdom (8) Netherlands (8)
12	84	037	**Fish preparations**	58	Thailand (20) China (10) Denmark (5)	Spain (4) Germany (4)
13	97	112	Alcoholic beverages	10	France (28) United Kingdom (16)	Italy (10) Spain (6)
14	101	054	**Fresh vegetables**	31	Netherlands (15) Spain (12) United States (9)	Mexico (9) Italy (7)
15	102	091	Margarine and shortening	25	Germany (16) Netherlands (11)	Belgium/Luxembourg (11) United States (7)
16	106	292	Crude vegetable materials	25	Netherlands (31) United States (7) Germany (5)	Italy (5) Denmark (5)
17	109	431	Processed animal and vegetable fats	48	Malaysia (25) Netherlands (12) Germany (10)	Indonesia (10) United States (6)
18	110	058	**Fruit preparations**	37	Brazil (11) United States (9) Germany (7)	Belgium/Luxembourg (6) Italy (6)
19	122	014	**Meat preparations**	23	Denmark (10) Belgium/Luxembourg (10)	United States (9) France (9)
20	123	024	**Cheese and curd**	2	France (19) Netherlands (18)	Germany (15) Denmark (9)

Source: See table 1.1.

  Note: See UNCTAD, *Handbook of Statistics* (table 4.4) for the main exporters of these products within the group of developing countries.

    a Product groups ranked by growth in export value, 1980–1998.

    b Bold characters indicate high-value products and/or items with an income elasticity of demand greater than one.

their world exports expanding even faster than those of a number of manufactures (annex A). Table 1.3 also shows that the share of developing countries in world exports is much higher for most of these products than for other market-dynamic agricultural products.

2. Market access

Differences in the speed of liberalization of markets can have a significant impact on the expansion of world trade in different products. When tariffs are the main forms of barriers to entry, across-the-board liberalization in the form of uniform tariff reductions is unlikely to result in significant differences in relative market access conditions and, hence, in the rates of expansion of trade in different products. By contrast, such differences can occur when: (i) trade liberalization involves non-tariff measures (NTMs) applied selectively to different products and/or suppliers; (ii) market access is liberalized in different degrees and speeds for different products; or (iii) selective and targeted contingent measures such as tariff-rate quotas or anti-dumping actions gain importance in commercial policy. All these features were prominent in the evolution of the world trading system during the period 1980–1998, and hence go a long way in explaining why world trade in different products has expanded at significantly different rates.

As discussed in *TDR 1993* (Part One, chap. II, sect. D), an important feature in the evolution of market access conditions was the persistent and, in some instances, growing resort to NTMs by industrialized countries during the period between the completion of the Tokyo Round (1979) and the Uruguay Round negotiations (1994). Voluntary export restraints (VERs), in particular, were increasingly applied to trade in steel, automobiles and consumer electronics. The growing number of NTMs, especially against unsophisticated manufactures, reinforced the prevailing patterns of market access which favoured primary commodities and high-tech products over middle-ground products that tend to gain importance in the early stages of industrialization. This pattern of trade controls remained largely unchanged throughout the 1980s; the little change that did occur only served to reinforce – rather than weaken – the bias against middle-ground products.[5]

---

[5] However, there were major increases in both frequency and coverage ratios of NTMs over the 1966–1986 period: food products recorded the highest overall increase in the frequency index; among manufactures, textiles and clothing, ferrous metals and transport equipment were the most affected products (Laird and Yeats, 1990).

There were two types of response by developing countries. Some of them shifted their manufacturing to products that enjoyed better market access. For example, the more advanced NIEs began focusing more on machinery and transport equipment for export (i.e. products that faced lower tariff and non-tariff barriers). Others changed to production and exports of goods for which they faced fewer market access barriers than other countries, rather than shifting to products that enjoyed better overall market access. For example, some countries with unfilled quotas under the Multi-Fibre Arrangement (MFA) increased their exports of clothing (Page, 1994).

As a result of the Uruguay Round agreements, changes in the conditions of market access have varied for different products as well as for different importing countries (WTO, 2001). In general, barriers to trade in industrial products have been lowered more than those to trade in agricultural products, and little has been achieved in terms of reducing trade-affecting subsidies in agriculture, particularly in the EU.

The major objective of the Uruguay Round Agreement on Agriculture was to establish a tariffs-only regime, so as to move away from a regime characterized by a large number of NTMs that were non-transparent in both their application and effects. Tariff rate quotas (TRQs) have been introduced to allow minimum access where there were no significant imports before the tariffication process, or to maintain current access levels where the tariffication would otherwise have reduced access.[6] They allow a certain quantity of imports to enter a market under a specific ("in-quota") tariff and then apply a higher ("out-of-quota") tariff to imports above the quota. The difference between the two tariff rates is frequently large: in those OECD countries that apply TRQs, they average 36 per cent and 120 per cent respectively. Most TRQs are concentrated in a few products, mainly fruits and vegetables, followed in importance by meat, cereals, dairy products and oilseeds.

While the Uruguay Round agreements achieved sizeable reductions in the use of NTMs, the phasing out period for existing NTMs differed significantly for different products: NTMs in agriculture, affecting mostly temperate zone food products (particularly grains and dairy products) exported mainly by developed countries, were to be phased out almost

---

[6] As the rules of tariffication also allowed for significant increases in tariffs, they remain high even after implementation of the agreed tariff reductions. Moreover, only limited progress has been made in reducing domestic support to agriculture and trade-distorting export subsidies. The account here draws on WTO (2001).

immediately, but those on textiles and clothing were given a transition period of 10 years, and VERs four years (Low and Yeats, 1995). These imbalances have been reinforced by the unequal incidence of VERs both across exporting countries and products. For example, as of 1992, of the 79 VERs outside agriculture and textiles and clothing, 69 involved Japan and the Republic of Korea as exporters, and they applied mainly to motor vehicles and consumer electronics (Finger and Schuknecht, 1999).

The failure of the Uruguay Round to impose a strong discipline over the use of anti-dumping practices may be one reason why they have become the most popular contingency protection actions employed by both developed and developing countries over the past few years. During the period 1995–1999, anti-dumping investigations increased rapidly, exceeding 1,200 cases, and most of the investigations were initiated against developing countries (WTO, 2001). Producers of base metals (principally steel), chemicals, machinery and electrical equipment, and plastics have frequently resorted to the use of anti-dumping actions (Miranda, Torres and Ruiz, 1998).

It is difficult to make a precise assessment of the impact of changes in market access conditions on the expansion of trade in different products. While most measures are the outcome of multilateral trade negotiations and are, hence, applied globally, some of the most restrictive practices, such as VERs and anti-dumping, are applied on a bilateral basis, sometimes with effects that work in opposite directions. Indeed the prohibition of VERs in the electronics sector has coincided with increased resort to anti-dumping. In some cases, increased resort to restrictions was a response to rapidly expanding market penetration of imports, while in others liberalization provided the impetus for such expansion.

Nevertheless, regarding broad product categories, available evidence suggests that trade liberalization has been limited and slow in agriculture, textiles and clothing; compared to other sectors, access to markets for these products continues to be much more restricted. Agricultural subsidies, particularly in the EU, have been largely responsible for restricting growth of exports of a number of agricultural commodities from developing countries. Moreover, the structure of TRQs has made market access particularly restrictive for agricultural products that have comparatively high income elasticities. These factors have certainly inhibited the expansion of world trade in agricultural products compared to manufactures. They also go a long way in explaining why, within the group of agricultural products, those with comparatively high income elasticities have not been able to outperform the others. In manufacturing, except in textiles and clothing, differences in the evolution of market access conditions are not large enough to explain the differences in the pace of expansion of trade in these products. Other factors affecting integration of markets, notably the growing importance of international production networks, appear to have played a greater role.

3. International production networks

a) The development of international production networks

The three product groups with the fastest and most stable growth rates over the past two decades (namely, parts and components for electrical and electronic goods, labour-intensive products, such as clothing, and finished goods with high R&D content) are also the ones most affected by the globalization of production processes through international production sharing.[7] Lower transport and communication costs and reduced trade and regulatory barriers have facilitated production sharing, which is generally concentrated in labour-intensive activities. These activities tend to involve technically unsophisticated production such as clothing or footwear industries; but they can also involve separation and location in different sites of labour-intensive segments of otherwise technologically complex production processes, such as those in the electronics or the automotive industry (Hummels, Rapoport and Yi, 1998). In such sectors, production sharing allows firms to exploit the comparative advantages specific to the production of particular components, including scale economies, and differences in labour costs across countries. In the electronics industry, components such as semiconductors are marketable commodities themselves, and can be used in a variety of end-products, such as computers, automobiles and household appliances. This allows firms to determine the location of the production of such components according to their own factor intensity and costs rather than the average factor intensity and cost of the end product.

---

[7] The phenomenon has alternatively been referred to as outsourcing, delocalization, fragmentation, intra-product specialization, intra-mediate trade, vertical specialization, and slicing the value chain, but it generally means the geographic separation of activities involved in producing a good (or service) across two or more countries. For a discussion of various issues associated with international production sharing, see, for example, Arndt and Kierzkowski (2001).

International production networks involve large TNCs which produce a standardized set of goods in several locations, or groups of small and medium-sized enterprises located in different countries and linked through international subcontracting; some of the more important areas of international production sharing organized along these lines are discussed in annex C. In the production of standardized goods, scale economies play a key role, and TNCs seek to increase profits by choosing locations with appropriate combinations of high labour productivity and low wage and infrastructure costs. This type of investment is highly mobile, as cost advantages can be easily lost due to wage increases or the emergence of more attractive new locations. Another characteristic of this type of international production network is that know-how and technology are usually kept within the TNCs themselves; they often enjoy monopolistic positions, as high costs of managing and coordinating such complex units constitute important barriers to entry into such sectors. Where international production networks are organized on the basis of subcontracting, the lead firm usually concentrates on R&D, design, finance, logistics and marketing, but it is not always involved in production activities. Such networks are typical of activities where labour-intensive segments of the production process can be separated from capital- and skill-/technology-intensive segments and located in low-wage areas.

It has been estimated, on the basis of input-output tables from a number of OECD and emerging-market countries, that trade based on specialization within vertical production networks accounts for up to 30 per cent of world exports, and that it has grown by as much as 40 per cent in the last 25 years (Hummels, Ishii and Yi, 2001). However, the size of international production sharing at the global level is difficult to trace over time, because international trade classifications prior to the second revision of SITC did not allow a distinction to be made between trade in final goods and trade in parts and components (Yeats, 2001). While this distinction is still not possible for most categories of products, it can be made for machinery and transport equipment, which accounts for about half of world trade in manufactures. Trade in parts and components is particularly important in the motor vehicle industry, computers and office machines, telecommunications equipment and electrical circuit equipment.[8] Moreover, trade in transistors and semiconductors[9] plays an important role in production sharing in East Asia (Ng and Yeats, 1999). The fact that trade in parts and components has grown strongly over the past few years, especially in the electronics industry, suggests that the rapid development of global production sharing has been a crucial factor in the rapid expansion of trade in these products as well as in the rising share of developing countries in these markets.

The dependence of manufacturing production and exports in developing countries on imported inputs such as capital and intermediate goods is not a new phenomenon. International product sharing constitutes a particular form of input-output relations between imports and exports that tends to raise the direct import content of exports relative to value added. In a sense, it has the same effect as trade liberalization, which often raises the direct as well as indirect import contents of exports by allowing easier access of foreign suppliers of capital and intermediate goods to domestic markets. However, international production networks promote a new pattern of trade, in that goods travel across several locations before reaching final consumers, and the total value of trade recorded in such products exceeds their value added by a considerable margin. Consequently, trade in such products can grow without a commensurate increase in their final consumption as production networks are extended across space.

The increased import content of exports has heightened the importance of the rules applied to determine the origin of traded goods, both as an instrument of commercial policy (regarding, for example, duty drawbacks and quantitative restrictions) and for recording trade flows on a product basis. Rules of origin follow the general concept that a product has its origin where the last "substantial transformation" took place. In practice, three main methods are used to determine whether substantial transformation has occurred. The first is the value-added measure, which refers to the percentage of value added created at the last stage of the production process. The second is the tariff heading criterion, whereby

---

[8] These product groups correspond to the SITC classification as follows: SITC 784 (parts and accessories for road motor vehicles), SITC 759 (parts and accessories for office machines and automatic data processing equipment), SITC 764 (telecommunications equipment and parts and accessories for telecommunications and sound recording and reproducing equipment), and SITC 772 (electrical apparatus for electrical circuits).

[9] This product group corresponds to SITC 776 (valves and tubes; photocells; diodes, transistors and similar semi-conductor devices; electronic microcircuits; and parts thereof).

origin is conferred if the activity in the exporting country results in a product classified under a different heading of the customs tariff classification than its intermediate inputs. This criterion is comparatively simple and predictable, but trade classification systems have not been designed with the objective of distinguishing substantial transformation. The third is the technical test, which determines, on a case-by-case basis, specific production activities that may confer originating status. Given that there are no internationally agreed standards, there is considerable room for interpretation and discretion by customs authorities in setting rules of origin. As a result, an importing country can vary rules of origin according to its trading partners and products.

b) Production sharing and preferential market access

The development of international production sharing has often been associated with the provision of preferential market access. While such a provision usually results in trade diversion, it tends to create trade when it is granted in the context of international production sharing. For instance, the MFA quota restrictions have had a crucial impact on production location and expansion of trade in textiles and clothing, particularly in Asia, where countries that had exhausted their quotas in industrial markets shifted production to new locations, using them as bases for exports (see annex C).

Other more specific arrangements affecting the volume of trade have involved mainly the United States and the EU. The United States implemented special tariff provisions as early as 1964 to encourage the use of its products in foreign assembly operations. These provisions have been continued, with some modification after 1988, under the production-sharing provisions of Chapter 98 of the Harmonized Tariff Schedule of the United States. They exempt from duty the value of components made in the United States that are returned to that country as parts of products assembled abroad. An additional provision was introduced in the context of NAFTA to allow duty-free treatment of Mexican value added in textile and apparel products assembled from fabric formed or cut in the United States (USITC, 1999a).

Outward processing trade (OPT) between the EU and its trading partners has been concentrated in labour-intensive sectors, particularly textiles and clothing.[10] The legislation on OPT goes back to the second

---

[10] The account here draws on ECE (1995), WTO (1998), and Graziani (2001).

extension of the MFA in 1982, when quotas for OPT were included for the first time in MFA III. The special treatment of textiles and clothing imports into the EU generally involves application of customs relief within certain import limits, or under surveillance arrangements provided for in the bilateral textile agreements concluded by the EU with a number of suppliers under the MFA. In practice, this usually means a combination of VERs and tariff suspension. It provides a preferential tariff quota on OPT re-imports, applied on a selective basis. The main beneficiaries of this scheme are some Mediterranean countries (Morocco, Tunisia and Turkey) and countries in Eastern Europe, especially the Baltic States. The scheme has been widely used: in Germany more than two thirds of the total trade in textiles and clothing with Central and Eastern European countries involves outward-processing operations.[11]

Preferential tariffs provided under regional trade agreements among developing countries, such as the Southern Common Market (MERCOSUR)[12] in Latin America and the ASEAN Free Trade Area (AFTA) in Asia, have also had a substantial impact on the expansion of trade in specific products among the countries involved. For example, the creation or consolidation of regional automobile industries in Latin America and in the Association of South-East Asian Nations (ASEAN), respectively, has given rise to substantial increases in FDI and intra-industry trade in these regions. In MERCOSUR, reciprocal preferential market access among member countries is aimed at developing an integrated regional industry and markets for automobiles; temporary protection is provided against non-members, until the industry can be substantially restructured with the help of FDI and integrated into the world market (annex C).

D.   Export dynamism and the potential for productivity growth

As noted above, the developmental effects of production and export of products differ according to their potential for demand and productivity growth. It is generally agreed that this potential is limited for primary commodities. However, there are also considerable differences

---

[11] For a detailed discussion of the OPT between the EU and Central European countries, see Baldone, Sdogati and Tajoli (2001).

[12] MERCOSUR comprises Argentina, Brazil, Paraguay and Uruguay (with agreements for a free trade area signed with Bolivia and Chile). ASEAN comprises Brunei Darussalam, Cambodia, Indonesia, Lao People's Democratic Republic, Malaysia, Myanmar, the Philippines, Singapore, Thailand and Viet Nam.

among manufactures in terms of their skill and technology intensity and productivity potentials.

A classification of products according to the mix of different skill, technology and capital intensity as well as scale characteristics results in five categories: primary commodities, labour- and resource-intensive manufactures, manufactures with low skill and technology intensity, manufactures with medium skill and technology intensity, and manufactures with high skill and technology intensity (*TDR 1996*: 116). Although the skill and technology intensity of a product does not necessarily indicate the productivity growth potential of the sector producing it, the relationship is close enough to focus the analysis on product categories based on their skill and technology intensity (box 1.1).

Box 1.1

Skill and technology intensity of products
and their potential for productivity growth

The product grouping used above reflects common perceptions regarding skill and technology intensities of their production processes. Since increased application of human capital and technology tends to raise labour productivity, such a classification can be expected to provide a reasonably good guide to sectoral differences in the potential for productivity growth. However, it should also be kept in mind that: (i) high productivity is not synonymous with high skill and technological intensity of production; and that (ii) productivity is influenced by a number of factors in addition to the mix of inputs and technology.

High value added per worker usually occurs in highly capital-intensive sectors or in traditional heavy manufacturing, while value added per worker can be lower in sectors that are highly technology-intensive. For example, in 1999 value added per worker in the United States was substantially higher in cigarette manufacturing, petroleum refining and automobile manufacturing ($1,944, $551 and $308 thousand respectively) than in aircraft manufacturing and computer and electronics (both around $170 thousand) (United States Census Bureau, 2001).

Since labour productivity is determined by a complex array of factors, high value added per worker does not always correspond to high technology intensity of production. Introduction of new management and organizational techniques, for example, can lead to substantial productivity increases in specific industries, as in the case of the lean production system introduced by Japanese automobile manufacturers. This gave them a substantial advantage over their competitors who continued to rely on the Fordist system of production. The ongoing debate on the sources of the growth of labour productivity in the United States during the second half of the 1990s also testifies to the complexity of this issue. While some stress the contribution to overall productivity growth resulting from the production of computers and semiconductors, others emphasize the large productivity gains that accrue from the use of information technology (see, for example, Oliner and Sichel, 2000; Gordon, 2000).

Total factor productivity (TFP) is an alternative measure to assess productivity and the link between technology intensity and economic performance. On the basis of this measure, sectors can be classified according to estimates of long-term rates of growth in TFP in large developed countries that are likely to be technological leaders (Choudhri and Hakura, 2000). However, this measure cannot be fully applied in the present context because it is based on the International Standard Industrial Classification (ISIC), while the SITC is usually applied in trade analyses. Nonetheless, allocating the products identified above as market-dynamic in world exports shows that almost all of them are in the group of high TFP-growth manufacturing sectors (textiles, wearing apparel and leather; chemicals and chemical products; and fabricated metal products, machinery and equipment), except for three primary commodities (silk, non-alcoholic beverages and cereals) and the group covering musical instruments, records and tapes.

Trade in all the five product categories listed above has expanded considerably since the mid-1980s. The expansion was particularly rapid for manufactures with high skill and technology intensity since 1993; trade in such products increased about fivefold between 1980 and 1998 (chart 1.3). Trade in labour- and resource-intensive products, as well as medium skill- and technology-intensive manufactures, has also grown faster than total non-fuel trade, but the difference has been fairly small. By contrast, trade in manufactures with low skill and technology intensity, and non-fuel primary commodities, has grown at a much slower rate than the average, particularly in recent years. Thus there has been a sharp fall in the share of non-fuel primary commodities in world trade, and a strong and sustained increase in the share of manufactures with high skill and technology intensity. Indeed, by the end of the 1990s, the share of the latter product category came to exceed the share of medium skill- and technology-intensive manufactures (table 1.4).

Chart 1.3

GROWTH OF EXPORTS OF DIFFERENT CLASSES OF GOODS, [a]
BY FACTOR INTENSITY, 1980-1998
(Index numbers, 1980 = 100)

A. World

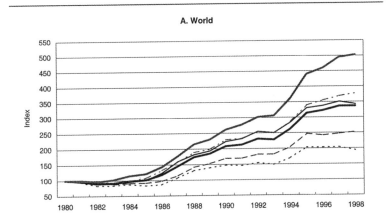

B. Developing countries

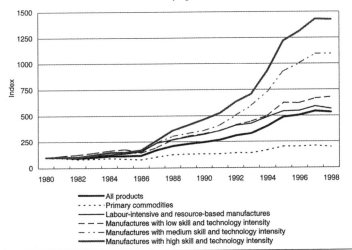

——— All products
· · · · · Primary commodities
——— Labour-intensive and resource-based manufactures
— — — Manufactures with low skill and technology intensity
— · — Manufactures with medium skill and technology intensity
▬▬▬ Manufactures with high skill and technology intensity

Source: See table 1.1
       [a] Excluding fuels

Table 1.4

**STRUCTURE OF EXPORTS[a] BY PRODUCT CATEGORIES ACCORDING TO
FACTOR INTENSITY, 1980 AND 1998**

(Percentage share)

Product category	Share in exports from developing countries		Share in world exports	
	1980	1998	1980	1998
Primary commodities	50.8	19.0	25.7	14.8
Labour-intensive and resource-based manufactures	21.8	23.2	14.7	15.0
Manufactures with low skill and technology intensity	5.8	7.3	10.1	7.6
Manufactures with medium skill and technology intensity	8.2	16.8	26.4	29.6
Manufactures with high skill and technology intensity	11.6	31.0	20.2	30.2

Source: See table 1.1.
Note: For the product classification see text.
   a Excluding fuels.

Except for non-fuel primary commodities, developing country exports of all product categories have grown more rapidly than world exports in the same product categories, and the difference has been higher the greater the skill and technology intensity of the products (chart 1.3). As a result, there has been a steep fall in the share of non-fuel primary commodities in total non-fuel exports of developing countries, from over 50 per cent in 1980 to under 20 per cent in 1998. The shares of labour- and resource-intensive products as well as low skill- and technology-intensive manufactures in total non-fuel exports of developing countries have remained largely unchanged, while those of medium and, in particular, high skill- and technology-intensive manufactures have increased strongly; in fact since the mid-1990s, the latter have accounted for the largest share in developing country exports.

Chart 1.4, based on SITC classification at 2- and 3-digit levels, shows that several goods in all product categories have experienced rapid growth in world exports in the past two decades, and, in this sense, dynamism is broad-based. However, all goods that combine rapid growth with a high share in world exports belong to the high and medium skill- and technology-intensive product categories. In developing countries, the products with a high share in total exports have also experienced the highest growth rates over the past two decades (chart 1.5). Thus the main

Chart 1.4

MARKET DYNAMISM OF INTERNATIONALLY TRADED GOODS,[a] BY FACTOR INTENSITY

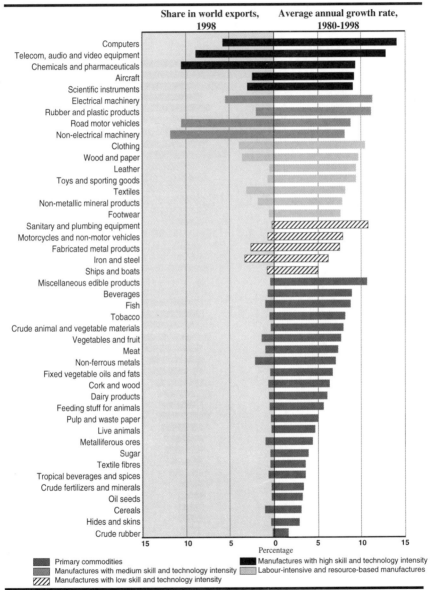

Share in world exports, 1998 | Average annual growth rate, 1980-1998

Computers
Telecom, audio and video equipment
Chemicals and pharmaceuticals
Aircraft
Scientific instruments
Electrical machinery
Rubber and plastic products
Road motor vehicles
Non-electrical machinery
Clothing
Wood and paper
Leather
Toys and sporting goods
Textiles
Non-metallic mineral products
Footwear
Sanitary and plumbing equipment
Motorcycles and non-motor vehicles
Fabricated metal products
Iron and steel
Ships and boats
Miscellaneous edible products
Beverages
Fish
Tobacco
Crude animal and vegetable materials
Vegetables and fruit
Meat
Non-ferrous metals
Fixed vegetable oils and fats
Cork and wood
Dairy products
Feeding stuff for animals
Pulp and waste paper
Live animals
Metalliferous ores
Sugar
Textile fibres
Tropical beverages and spices
Crude fertilizers and minerals
Oil seeds
Cereals
Hides and skins
Crude rubber

15   10   5   0   5   10   15
Percentage

■ Primary commodities
■ Manufactures with medium skill and technology intensity
▧ Manufactures with low skill and technology intensity
■ Manufactures with high skill and technology intensity
□ Labour-intensive and resource-based manufactures

Source: See table 1.1.
Note: Both product groups and subgroups are ranked in decreasing order by their average rate of growth during the period 1980-1998. For some of the product groups listed in this chart, the definition differs from that used elsewhere in this study. These are: "computers", comprising here computers and office equipment, and parts of computers and office machines (SITC 75); "telecom equipment", comprising here telecommunications, audio and video equipment (SITC 76), and transistors and semiconductors (SITC 776); and "electrical machinery", comprising here electrical power machinery, electrical apparatus and appliances, and parts thereof (SITC 771-775), but excluding transistors and semiconductors (SITC 776).
[a] Excluding fuels.

Chart 1.5

MARKET DYNAMISM OF DEVELOPING COUNTRY EXPORTS,ᵃ BY FACTOR INTENSITY

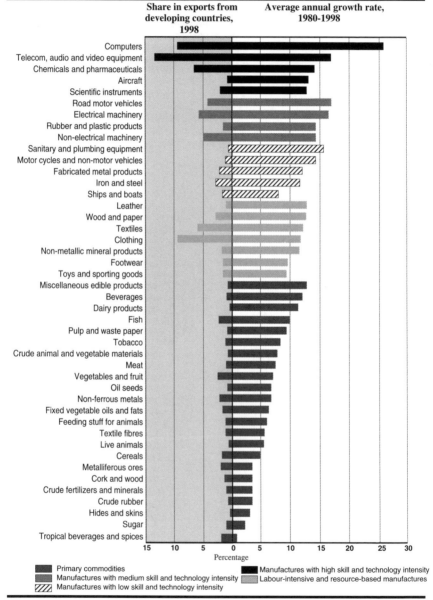

Source: See table 1.1.
Note: See chart 1.4.
     ᵃ Excluding fuels.

exports of developing countries are concentrated in computers and office equipment; telecommunications, audio and video equipment and semiconductors; and clothing. All these products involve labour-intensive processes, which suggests that the increased importance of global production sharing has been a crucial determinant of the growth of their exports.

Thus, the analysis of growth in exports of different product categories suggests that there are market-dynamic products in all categories, including some primary commodities. However, exports of products from the high skill- and technology-intensive group have grown most rapidly over the past two decades. Perhaps the most striking finding is that the higher the skill and technology contents of exports, the faster is the growth rate of exports of developing countries compared to growth in world trade. However, this does not necessarily imply that there has been a rapid and sustained technological upgrading in exports of developing countries. First, their rapid growth in exports of skill- and technology-intensive goods started from a relatively small base in the early 1980s. Secondly – and more importantly – since the involvement of developing countries in exports of such products is usually limited to the labour-intensive processes in these sectors in the context of international production sharing, simple measures of growth in gross export values are poor guides for an assessment of the nature of participation of developing countries in world trade.

E. Variations among developing countries

The main exporters of the most dynamic products in world markets are the industrialized countries. Among developing countries only some of the East Asian economies have managed to supply the world markets with a significant quantity of these dynamic products. Most of the other developing regions do not appear to have been able to participate in this process.[13]

The most market-dynamic products in the exports from developed countries, developing countries as a group, and for regional subgroups are given in table 1.A2 in annex A. The table shows that the 15 fastest growing exports of industrial countries are among the 20 most market-dynamic products in world markets. By contrast, only 8 of the 20 most

---

[13] For the composition of the country groups used here, see UNCTAD (2000). For a more detailed description of export structure of individual or various groups of developing countries, see Mayer, Butkevicius and Kadri (2002).

rapidly growing exports of developing countries are among the 20 most dynamic products in world markets. While these include the four fastest growing products in world trade, this is largely due to the increased participation of developing countries in the labour-intensive segments of production of high-tech electronic goods in the context of international production sharing. Similarly, the growing importance of production outsourcing to developing countries appears to be the main reason why products from the clothing sector are among the fastest growing exports of industrial countries rather than developing countries.

It is perhaps surprising that only 3 of the 20 most dynamic products in world markets (table 1.1) are among the 20 fastest growing exports of the *first-tier NIEs*; these are computers, parts of computers and office machines, and optical instruments. However, this is only an indication that these economies do not provide attractive locations for labour-intensive processes in the production of many dynamic products with high skill and technology context. By contrast, 5 items from the chemical industry are among the 20 most rapidly expanding exports of the first-tier NIEs, and finished products of the motor vehicle industry also rank comparatively high. Textiles rank much higher than clothing in their exports, suggesting that the first-tier NIEs have, over the years, succeeded in upgrading from comparatively labour-intensive clothing to more sophisticated textiles.

Computers, parts of computers and office machines, optical instruments, and telecommunications, audio and video equipment are the most important subgroups in the dynamic exports of the *ASEAN-4* (Indonesia, Malaysia, the Philippines and Thailand). But it is noteworthy that passenger motor vehicles are also among the 20 fastest growing exports from these countries. The most dynamic products in exports from *South Asia* belong to a wide variety of product groups, but there are significantly fewer electronics products than in East Asia. The absence of any product from the clothing sector is also notable.

As a group, countries in *South America* appear to have been largely excluded from dynamic exports in world markets. Only 2 of the group's fastest growing exports are among the 20 most dynamic products in world trade: non-alcoholic beverages and knitted fabrics. Products that are subject to global production sharing are not among the most dynamic exports from South America. The region does not participate significantly in global production sharing because of such factors as greater geographical distance from the developed countries that have been the most active in such activities, high wages compared to productivity, and inadequate infrastructure. Countries in the region have relied on their abundance of natural resources to strongly expand their primary exports: their 6 most dynamic products are primary commodities, and among the 20 fastest growing exports of South America there is a total of 9 primary commodities.[14]

Turning to the experiences of individual countries, a comparison of the shares of the four fastest growing product groups in the exports of the major developing countries reveals the following:[15]

- *Electronic and electrical goods* are the leading exports of all four first-tier NIEs (though they are less important in the Republic of Korea than in the others), as well as of Malaysia, the Philippines and Thailand. They also play an important role in China, Costa Rica and Mexico.

- *Textiles and labour-intensive manufactures, in particular clothing,* are important in China, Costa Rica, India, Mexico, Morocco, the Philippines, the Republic of Korea, Taiwan Province of China, Thailand, Tunisia and Turkey.

- *Transport equipment, in particular passenger motor cars and other motor vehicles,* is the only group of finished goods from technologically complex industries that features among the leading exports of several developing countries, in particular Argentina, Brazil, Mexico and the Republic of Korea. However, only in the Republic of Korea do these exports reflect nationally grown production activities.

- *Primary commodities and, in particular, supply-dynamic primary commodities* are of some importance in India, Indonesia, Malaysia, the Philippines, Thailand, Tunisia and Turkey, and are very important for a number of countries in South America and for Morocco.

---

[14] For countries in Africa and Central America and the Caribbean, the wide range of product groups of their 20 most dynamic export products makes it difficult to detect a distinct pattern, due, in part, to the heterogeneity of countries in the region.

[15] In this comparison, only the 20 countries with the fastest export growth during the period 1980–1998 and with total export earnings in excess of $5 billion in 1998 are included. Without the latter condition, the group of 20 countries with the fastest rates of export growth would feature a number of very small countries such as Benin, Bhutan, Cambodia, Djibouti, Equatorial Guinea, Lao People's Democratic Republic, Lesotho, Maldives and Seychelles.

No doubt, many country-specific factors, including size and resource endowments, have influenced the export composition and dynamics of these countries. However, there is a distinctive regional pattern in the different experiences of countries, which suggests that geography has played an important role. Products involved in global production sharing are important only in the exports of countries which are geographically close to one of the main developed country markets, namely the United States, the EU and Japan. By contrast, they are not significant exports of countries geographically distant from these markets.

However, this does not mean that international production networks are contained within regions. In this respect too, East Asian economies appear to be different from countries in other regions in that their integration in international production networks is much broader than that of countries geographically close to the United States or the EU. Enterprises in East Asia operate regional production networks but they also export to the United States and Europe. By contrast, countries in Eastern Europe tend to concentrate on production sharing with the EU, and enterprises in countries close to the United States, notably Mexico, tend to be included in production networks only with the United States.

F. Exports, industrialization and growth

1. International production networks, trade and industrialization

How are these varying performances of countries in world trade reflected in their overall economic performance, particularly in industrialization and growth? In general, closer integration of countries into the global trading system through greater liberalization and openness is expected to increase the share of international trade in domestic economic activity. It does so by expanding the size of the traded goods sectors relative to the rest of the economy and by shifting resources from protected import-substituting industries – thereby lowering production in such industries – to export-oriented industries. As a result, imports and exports tend to increase at any given level of resource utilization. The participation in global production networks reinforces this process. Indeed, most developing countries which have rapidly opened up their economies in recent years have experienced a significant increase in the ratio of trade to income. On some accounts, such a reshuffling of resources according to comparative advantages yields significant efficiency gains and welfare benefits. However, the benefits are extremely difficult to quantify and substantiate, giving rise to considerable debate over the potential benefits of the Uruguay Round agreements. In any case, these benefits tend to be one-off. What matters, from a development point of view, is whether closer integration and faster expansion of imports and exports result in a faster rate of growth and convergence of incomes with industrial countries.

The mechanisms linking exports to economic growth and industrialization in developing countries have been described in considerable detail in previous *TDRs* in relation to the evolution of the East Asian NIEs and to the problems encountered in commodity-dependent African countries in accelerating accumulation and growth.[16] These linkages vary according to the stage of development. In the earliest stage, access to world markets provides a "vent for surplus" for developing countries, allowing them to take advantage of formerly underutilized land and labour to produce larger volumes of primary commodities, the surplus of which can be exported. This considerably helps raise income and activity, even when value added per worker is relatively low, and it provides the foreign exchange needed for imports and investment. The next step is to begin diversification and processing of the commodities for export. However, the possibilities for accelerating development through deepening and diversification in the primary sector are limited. For the vast majority of developing countries, sustained economic growth requires a shift in the structure of economic activity towards manufactured goods. In most countries, manufacturing industries are established initially for traditional labour-intensive products, which are the obvious candidates for the first generation of manufactured exports. As incomes rise and the surplus labour is absorbed, rising labour costs and the entry of lower-cost producers progressively erode the competitiveness of many labour-intensive manufactures. This leads to a new challenge, that of upgrading industrial activity so as to produce more sophisticated manufactures. This move away from resource-dependent and labour-intensive activities towards more technology- and skill-intensive activities underlies the success of post-war industrialization in East Asia, mainly in Japan, the Republic of Korea and Taiwan Province of China. As discussed in considerable detail in earlier *TDRs*, this success was based on a mix of trade and industrial policies and an approach to FDI that were substantially different from the ones adopted by a large

---

[16] See, in particular, *TDR 1996* (Part Two, chap. II); *TDR 1997* (Part Two, chap. II); and *TDR 1998* (Part Two, chap. IV).

number of developing countries either in the previous era of import-substitution, or during the more recent shift to big-bang liberalization.[17]

Indeed, the evidence examined above suggests that, with the exception of a few East Asian NIEs, which have reached income levels as high as or even higher than many industrialized countries, the exports of developing countries are still largely based on the exploitation of natural resources or unskilled labour. Evidence suggesting a rapid expansion of technology- and skill-intensive exports from developing countries is misleading, since these countries are mostly involved in the low-skill assembly stages of the production chain. The shift from primary products to a first generation of manufactures does not, for the most part, represent a shift towards more sophisticated activities. On the contrary, the production of certain primary products may be more skill-/capital-intensive and have more linkages to the rest of the economy than some unskilled or semi-skilled assembly activities.

This is not to deny that the growing importance of international production sharing in products such as computers and office equipment, semiconductors and communications equipment offers new opportunities to developing countries with considerable surplus labour to utilize it more fully, and hence to raise their per capita income. Participation in such production networks can also create some impetus to development by broadening the range of sectors in which developing countries can base their industrialization efforts. It can indeed be argued that since product-specific characteristics of production processes allow them to be partitioned into various "slices", it is no longer necessary for producers to master entire production chains and to organize them within single firms, which would be beyond the means of most developing countries. They can thus focus on mastering just one facet of production and a limited subset of all the activities involved in making a final product. This is likely to entail large savings in learning costs and can allow small and medium-sized domestic companies to coexist with large TNCs. Given relative factor endowments, developing countries may begin by creating competency in the more labour-intensive components of complex products and gradually progressing to more skill- and technology-intensive activities.

---

[17] For a discussion of policies in East Asia, see *TDR 1994* (Part Two, chap. I) and *TDR 1996* (Part Two). For a critical assessment of big-bang liberalization, see *TDR 1997* (Part Two, chaps. II and IV) and *TDR 1999* (chap. VI); and for import-substitution policies in Africa, see *TDR 1998* (Part Two, chaps. IV and V).

However, the participation of developing countries in such production chains is not without problems and risks. First, increasing value added through technological upgrading and productivity growth in the context of international production sharing may prove to be more difficult than in self-contained, independent industries. Second, growing competition among developing countries to attract FDI in order to enter such markets may lead to problems relating to fallacy of composition and provoke a race to the bottom.

As illustrated by the cases examined in annex C, participation in the labour-intensive segments of international production chains does not automatically bring the technological spillovers needed to move up in the production chain. There are certainly successful examples of import substitution in the context of international production sharing, involving a move from assembly of imported components to their domestic production. One such example is the development of domestic capacity in textiles and clothing in the Republic of Korea, described in annex C. Another is the computer industry in Taiwan Province of China, which is the most broadly-based industry in that sector in Asia outside Japan. That economy has diversified beyond core personal computer (PC)-related products into a variety of high-growth market segments and improved its domestic production capabilities for a number of high value-added components, moving even beyond manufacturing into a range of higher-end, knowledge-intensive support services (Ernst, 2000). Similarly, Singapore has been rather successful in targeting specific industries for promotion, and in using TNC-controlled assets in efforts to upgrade.[18]

However, such success stories appear to be exceptions. Generally, developing countries participating in international production chains are not involved in the skill- and technology-intensive parts of the overall production process. Where the local suppliers' base is developed, it is mainly the foreign-owned suppliers, rather than national firms, that manufacture the most sophisticated key components.[19] This can hinder development of domestic supply capability and carries the risk of the host country getting locked in to its current structure of comparative

---

[18] See Lall (1995, 1998). For a comparison of policies related to FDI and TNCs among the East Asian NIEs, see *TDR 1996* (Part Two, chap. II).

[19] This appears to be the case even in Malaysia, which has a more developed local suppliers' base in electrical equipment and electronics industry than many other countries participating in international production networks in these products, including Mexico and Thailand (Mortimore, Romijn and Lall, 2000: 71). Foreign ownership of domestic suppliers is also important in the automotive industry (UNCTAD, 2001, box IV.2: 132).

advantage, with its stress on unskilled or semi-skilled labour-intensive activities, thereby delaying the exploitation of potential comparative advantage in higher-tech stages of production. It can be a major problem for most developing economies involved in international production networks. Since they are not at rudimentary stages of development with large amounts of underutilized labour, but rather middle-income economies, which have been successful in early stages of industrialization based on labour and natural resources, they now need to undertake rapid upgrading in order to advance further in industrialization and development. Indeed, this pattern of participation in international production networks for manufacturing exports has been causing concern in recent years, even in some of the East Asian countries which have been more successful in exploiting various advantages associated with TNCs. It has been noted that these concerns relate to:

> ... the costs to local businesses of the bias towards export-led manufacturing and foreign investment. ... With the partial exceptions of Taiwan [Province of China] and Singapore (which are heavily engaged in 'original equipment manufacturing' production for foreign firms), East Asia's economic bias towards manufactured exports has delivered neither the quantity nor the depth of backward linkages that planners and local capital desired. Except for Taiwan [Province of China], manufacturing exports are still dominated by foreign firms' branch plants with unsatisfying linkages either to the local market or to local firms. (*Oxford Analytica Brief*, 2002: 1–2)

It is also notable that most of these countries remain attractive locations for low-wage, labour-intensive segments of international production networks for manufacturing exports by accepting a large number of foreign workers who, according to some estimates, constitute up to 25 per cent of the labour force in countries like Malaysia and Singapore (*Oxford Analytica Brief*, 2002). A similar picture was drawn by the Economic Commission for Latin America and the Caribbean (UNCTAD/ECLAC) concerning recent efforts in Latin America, where

> ... many countries that improved their international competitiveness through FDI in manufactures not based on natural resources, generated very weak linkages between the local economy and the export platforms. In general, the lack of linkage promotion strategy was highlighted, especially in

the cases of Mexico, Costa Rica and Honduras, where the success in exports has not been followed by a similar development of the local industrial base. (UNCTAD/ECLAC, 2002)

According to the ECLAC study, efforts aimed simply at attracting FDI through macroeconomic stability and passive investment policies run the risk of locking static advantages inside export platforms with minimal linkages to the domestic industry.

This risk of getting locked in is particularly high where trade flows are based on preferential market access that requires production inputs to be sourced from a developed country partner. Moreover, the increased production complementarities between developed and developing countries imply that a greater share of developing country production and exports comes to depend on the decisions and performance of foreign firms and countries. This reduces policy autonomy in developing countries regarding the formulation of development strategies that emphasize national capabilities and goals. Thus the geographic dispersion of production activities may lead to less, rather than more, technology transfer. The spillovers from engaging in subcontracting or hosting affiliates of TNCs are reduced because the package of technology and skills required at any one site becomes narrower and because cross-border backward and forward linkages are strengthened at the expense of domestic ones. Furthermore, when only a small part of the production chain is involved, out-contractors and TNCs have a wider choice of potential sites – since these activities take on a more footloose character – which strengthens their bargaining position vis-à-vis the host country. This can engender excessive and unhealthy competition among developing countries as they begin to offer TNCs increasing fiscal and trade-related concessions in order to compensate for the shifting competitiveness from one group of developing countries to another; it can thereby aggravate the inequalities in the distribution of gains from international trade and investment between TNCs and developing countries.

Indeed, technological upgrading can be more difficult for economies that are used by TNCs primarily as bases for exports to third markets than for economies where FDI is of the market-seeking, tariff-jumping kind. Since the latter form of FDI is more dependent on the domestic economy, it gives the host country government greater bargaining power for using FDI selectively to ensure that it will create spillovers and linkages with domestic industry in the context of a broader industrialization strategy. Most examples of successful use of FDI in industrialization and technological progress, including some of the cases mentioned above, are from countries that have exploited this advantage effectively.

These features of TNC-driven international production networks were noted by Paul Streeten in the 1970s, when the trend first became apparent:

> In one sense, the doctrine of comparative advantage seems to be vindicated, though in a manner quite different from that normally envisaged. It is foreign, not domestic, capital, know-how and management that are highly mobile internationally and that are combined with plentiful, immobile domestic semi-skilled labour. Specialisation between countries is not by commodities according to relative factor endowments, but by factors of production: the poor countries specialising in low-skilled labour, leaving the rewards for capital, management and know-how to the foreign owners of these scarce but internationally mobile factors. The situation is equivalent to one in which *labour itself* rather than the *product of labour* is exported. For the surplus of the product of labour over the wage ... accrues abroad. ... Since the firms operate in oligopolistic and oligopsonistic markets, cost advantages are not necessarily passed on to consumers in lower prices or to workers in higher wages, and the profits then accrue to the parent firms. The continued operation of this type of international specialisation depends upon the continuation of substantial wage differentials ...

> The packaged nature of the contribution of the MNEs, usually claimed as its characteristic blessing, is in this context the cause of the unequal international distribution of the gains from trade and investment. If the package broke or leaked, some of the rents and monopoly rewards would spill over into the host country. But if it is secured tightly, only the least scarce and weakest factor in the host country derives an income from the operations of the MNEs, unless bargaining power is used to extract a share of these other incomes. (Streeten, 1993: 356–357)

A strategy of development based on participation in labour-intensive processes in global production networks is substantially different from the successful post-war experiences of industrialization in East Asia, where the location of countries in the international division of labour resulted from well-targeted trade and industrial policies. Such policies were particularly important in the first-tier NIEs, notably the Republic of Korea and Taiwan Province of China, as they moved out of labour-intensive manufactures and into more technologically sophisticated and capital-intensive activities. As part of a strategic approach to FDI inflows, their policy makers sought to maximize the benefits in foreign exchange and technology that they could extract from TNCs, and to ensure that these complemented – rather than substituted – efforts to strengthen domestic capacity.[20]

2. Trade in manufactures, value added, and growth

The discussion above suggests that the recent success of many developing countries in expanding their manufactured exports and improving their share in world trade, particularly in what appear to be high-tech products, cannot be taken at face value. In fact, the increased import content of domestic production and consumption brought about by rapid trade liberalization, together with the greater participation of developing countries in import-dependent, labour-intensive, low value-added processes in international production networks, implies that such increases in the manufacturing exports of developing countries may have taken place without commensurate increases in incomes and value added. Chart 1.6 compares the evolution of manufacturing trade and value added in the G-7 countries with a group of seven of the more advanced developing countries (D-7) for which data are available. This comparison is revealing, since the G-7 accounts for almost half of world trade and two thirds of global income, and the D-7 for about 60 per cent of developing

---

[20] See *TDR 1996* (Part Two, chap. I).

country trade and 40 per cent of developing country GDP.[21] It yields a number of results:

- A significant difference between the two groups is that manufacturing value added consistently exceeds manufacturing trade in developed countries, but the opposite is true for developing countries.

- In both groups, manufacturing value added tended to fall relative to manufacturing trade over the past two decades, but the decline was much more pronounced in developing countries; in the G-7 countries the ratio of manufacturing value added to manufactured exports fell from some 225 per cent in the early 1980s to 180 per cent in the late 1990s, compared to developing countries where it declined from 75 per cent to 55 per cent over the same period.

- In developing countries, manufacturing exports and imports were broadly at the same levels until the end of the 1980s, when imports started to grow much faster than exports, while in industrial countries manufactured exports constantly exceeded imports.

- While the ratios of manufactured value added and exports to GDP remained broadly unchanged in the industrialized countries, in the developing countries the ratios of manufactured exports to GDP rose steeply, but there was no significant upward trend in the ratio of manufacturing value added to GDP.

There are, however, significant differences among developing countries regarding the relation between manufactured trade and value added, reflecting, in large part, differences in their pattern of industrialization and integration into the global trading system (chart 1.7).[22] Of these countries, the Republic of Korea stands alone, with a production-trade configuration similar to that of the major industrial

---

[21] The original data provided by Nicita and Olarreaga (2001) were based on the definition of manufactures used in the International Standard Industrial Classification (ISIC). Data in chart 1.6 are based on the definition of manufactures used in the Standard International Trade Classification (SITC); the conversion of the former to the latter required an adjustment, involving the exclusion of processed foods, fuels and minerals. Data for China are available only from 1986 onwards. Without China it is possible to construct time series for manufacturing trade and value added for the period 1981–1996. The overall picture, however, is broadly the same.

[22] The figures in the Industrial Statistics database of the United Nations Industrial Development Organization (UNIDO) as well as those given in Nicita and Olarreaga (2001) show a strong spike for Chinese manufacturing value added for 1993. This appears to reflect, in large part, the effect of the devaluation of the currency, since value added in chart 1.7 is measured in current dollars.

Chart 1.6

**TRADE IN MANUFACTURES AND VALUE ADDED IN MANUFACTURING FOR
SELECTED GROUPS OF ECONOMIES, 1981-1996**
(Billions of dollars)

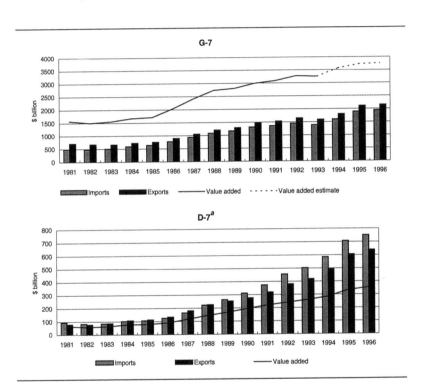

Source: UNCTAD secretariat calculations, based on Nicita and Olarreaga (2001).

Note: Manufactured goods as defined by SITC. Value added data for the period after 1993 was not available for all countries. The estimates for G-7 value added during the period 1994-1996 are based on data for four countries (Canada, Japan, the United Kingdom and the United States) and on the assumption that value added for the G-7 as a whole grew at the same rate during that period as it did for these countries.

ᵃ Hong Kong (China), Malaysia, Mexico, Republic of Korea, Singapore, Taiwan Province of China, and Turkey.

countries. In all first-tier NIEs, except Hong Kong (China), manufacturing value added rose as fast as, or faster than, both manufactured imports and exports over the past two decades. Indeed, Hong Kong (China) stands at the other extreme; it appears as an entrepôt, with much of its earnings coming from intermediary services. Its manufacturing value added is only a fraction of its manufactured exports, and the gap between the two has been widening. In contrast to the three other economies in the first-tier NIEs, Hong Kong (China) has pursued a laissez-faire approach to FDI. It is the least successful of the East Asian NIEs in upgrading, but its special circumstances have allowed it to grow and prosper.[23]

In both Malaysia and Mexico, manufactured imports and exports exceed value added by a large margin. As noted above, in both countries exports have high direct import contents due to their close involvement in international production networks. For example, one recent study estimated that in Mexico imports for further processing constitute as much as one half to two thirds of the total sales of affiliates of United States TNCs in industries such as computers and office equipment, electronic equipment, and transport equipment.[24] In Mexico, growth in manufacturing value added has been negligible compared to the surge in its manufactured imports and exports. Malaysia, however, has had a very strong growth in manufacturing value added in the past two decades, in part due to the establishment of local suppliers' networks based on foreign ownership.

By contrast, in both Turkey and China, on average, manufacturing value added has exceeded manufactured exports. Turkey does not participate significantly in international production networks, and its manufacturing exports have a low direct import content. However, its manufacturing imports exceed exports by a wide margin, partly due to its high degree of dependence on imported capital goods and intermediate inputs and a growing share of consumer goods imports in total spending. As noted above, China participates in labour-intensive segments of international production networks, and the direct import content of its exports of electrical and electronic goods is high. But it also has large

---

[23] For a detailed analysis, see *TDR 1996* (Part Two, chap. II).

[24] The fact that this share is much higher – particularly in electronic equipment – than that of affiliates in other locations with similar labour productivity and average incomes is probably due mainly to Mexico's favourable tax policies for TNCs, preferential market access provisions under NAFTA, and geographic proximity to the United States (Hanson, Mataloni and Slaughter, 2002).

traditional labour-intensive export industries with relatively high value added and little direct import content. Furthermore, China has so far avoided rapid import liberalization (except for exports), and its imports of manufactured consumer goods remain low.

Economic size is an important determinant of the degree of trade orientation, and smaller countries tend to have a high trade-income ratio. However, success in industrialization and the pattern of integration into the global trading system also matter, as can be seen by comparing the relative evolution of trade and value added for the Republic of Korea and Mexico (chart 1.7), two economies that are identical in size (with a 3 per cent income weighting in OECD). Comparing Turkey with Mexico, even though it is smaller in economic size (less than 2 per cent in OECD income weighting), the Turkish manufacturing value added exceeds its manufactured exports by almost 50 per cent, whereas for Mexico manufacturing value added is around one third of its exports (and imports).

These results also suggest that a country's growing share in world manufacturing trade does not necessarily imply a corresponding increase in its share in world manufacturing output and income. However, comprehensive and consistent data on manufacturing value added are not available to allow worldwide comparisons in these respects. Table 1.5 shows data, assembled from various sources, on the shares of developed and developing economies in world manufacturing trade and production over the past two decades.[25] An important observation from the table is that, while the share of developed countries in world manufacturing exports fell between 1980 and 1997, their share in world manufacturing income rose significantly. In other words, in relative terms, industrial countries appear to be trading less but earning more in manufacturing activity.

Developing economies' shares both in world manufacturing exports and value added show a sharp increase during the same period, but growth in exports is much stronger than in value added. All Asian economies in table 1.5, as well as Turkey, increased their shares in world manufacturing exports, while in Latin America this was true only for

---

[25] In table 1.5 the data on value added are based on the definition of manufactures used in ISIC, while the data on exports are based on the definition of manufactures used in SITC. However, calculating the share in world manufactured exports based on the definition of manufactures used in industrial statistics yields very similar results for countries for which comprehensive data are available.

Chart 1.7

TRADE IN MANUFACTURES AND VALUE ADDED IN MANUFACTURING OF SELECTED DEVELOPING ECONOMIES
(Billions of dollars)

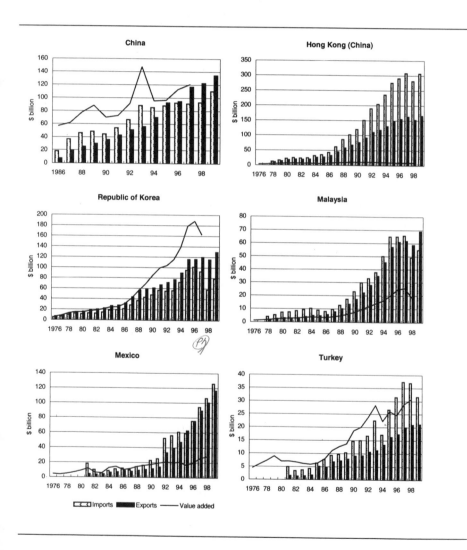

Source: UNCTAD secretariat calculations, based on Nicita and Olarreaga (2001).

Note: Manufactures as defined by SITC.

Table 1.5

SHARE OF SELECTED REGIONAL GROUPS AND DEVELOPING ECONOMIES IN WORLD
EXPORTS OF MANUFACTURES AND MANUFACTURING VALUE ADDED, 1980 AND 1997

(Percentage share)

Region/economy	Share in world exports of manufactures		Share in world manufacturing value added	
	1980	*1997*	*1980*	*1997*
Developed countries	82.3	70.9	64.5	73.3
Developing countries	10.6	26.5	16.6	23.8
Latin America	1.5	3.5	7.1	6.7
Argentina	0.2	0.2	0.9	0.9
Brazil	0.7	0.7	2.9	2.7
Chile	0.0	0.1	0.2	0.2
Mexico	0.2	2.2	1.9	1.2
South and East Asia	6.0^a	16.9	7.3	14.0
NIEs	5.1	8.9	1.7	4.5
Hong Kong (China)	0.2	0.6	0.3	0.2
Republic of Korea	1.4	2.9	0.7	2.3
Singapore	0.9	2.6	0.1	0.4
Taiwan Province of China	1.6	2.8	0.6	1.6
ASEAN-4	0.6	3.6	1.2	2.6
Indonesia	0.1	0.6	0.4	1.0
Malaysia	0.2	1.5	0.2	0.5
Philippines	0.1	0.5	0.3	0.3
Thailand	0.2	1.0	0.3	0.8
China	1.1^b	3.8	3.3	5.8
India	0.4	0.6	1.1	1.1
Turkey	0.1	0.5	0.4	0.5

Source: UNCTAD secretariat calculations, based on UNIDO, *Handbook of Industrial Statistics* (various issues); UNIDO,
International Yearbook of Industrial Statistics, various issues; World Bank, *World Development Indicators 2000* (table 4.3);
UN/DESA, *Commodity Trade Statistics* database; and UN/DESA, *Monthly Bulletin of Statistics* (various issues).

Note: Calculations in current dollars. Value-added data are based on the definition of manufactures used in industrial statistics,
while export data are based on the definition of manufactures used in trade statistics. However, calculating the share in
world manufactured exports based on the definition of manufactures used in industrial statistics yields very similar results
for countries for which comprehensive data are available.

a Excluding China.
b 1984.

Mexico. It is notable that the other major economies in Latin America, notably Argentina and Brazil, which do not participate significantly in international production networks, have been unable to increase their shares in world manufacturing exports. Similarly, with the exception of Hong Kong (China) and the Philippines, all East Asian countries increased their shares in world manufacturing value added, but none in Latin America was able to do so. Briefly, of the economies examined here, none of those which pursued rapid liberalization of trade and investment over the past two decades achieved a significant increase in its share in world manufacturing income, although some of them experienced a rapid growth in manufacturing exports.

There is thus little correlation between the growth of exports and growth of value added for any of the developing economies listed in table 1.5. Hong Kong (China), Mexico, the Philippines and Turkey are among the countries that recorded the largest increases in their shares in world manufactured exports, but the shares of Hong Kong (China) and Mexico in world manufacturing value added actually fell, that of the Philippines stagnated, while that of Turkey registered only a moderate increase. It is particularly notable that between 1980 and 1997 Mexico's share in world manufactured exports rose tenfold, while its share in world manufacturing valued added fell by more than one third, and its share in world income (at current dollars) by about 13 per cent. By contrast, the Republic of Korea, Singapore and Taiwan Province of China recorded the highest gains in terms of their share in world manufacturing income, without concomitant increases in their shares in world manufactured exports. While China had an outstanding performance both in trade and growth, the increase in its share in world manufacturing value added is less impressive than its share in manufactured trade. This is also true for the second-tier NIEs, that have succeeded in improving their shares in both world manufacturing trade and value added in the past two decades.

Moreover, in countries that participate extensively in international production networks through FDI, an important part of the value added in TNCs accrues to foreign firms as profits. In East Asia this is true for both Malaysia (*TDR 1999*: 120–123 and table 5.6) and China (see chapter V).

G. Conclusions

For more than a decade, world trade has been growing, on average, faster than world income as a result of rapid integration. However, integration has progressed at differential rates in different markets. While world trade in a number of products has expanded at double digit rates, in some others it has stagnated or declined in absolute terms. To a certain extent, this is due to differences in income elasticities and the pace of product innovation in different sectors. But it also reflects, in part, structural shifts in the pattern of competitiveness, particularly the emergence of new players among developing countries in a number of sectors.

It is also possible that policies governing market access for both goods and FDI may have had a more decisive influence over the evolution of trade in different products. While continued barriers in industrial countries have impeded growth of trade in many areas of export interest to developing countries, rapid liberalization in these countries has helped expand trade in skill- and technology-intensive manufactures in which more advanced countries have a competitive edge. The increased mobility of capital, together with continued restrictions on the mobility of labour, has extended the reach of international production networks. This has accelerated trade in a number of sectors where production chains can be split up and located in different countries. Commercial policies in industrial countries have helped this process by granting preferential market access to goods produced by the foreign assembly operations of their TNCs as well as to goods containing inputs originating in their countries. Policies in developing countries have also contributed by offering various incentives to FDI and encouraging TNCs to operate in their territories with minimum restrictions.

The evidence examined above shows that the benefits of integration and expansion of international trade depend on the modalities of countries' participation in the trading system and on how trade is linked to domestic economic activity. An important conclusion that emerges is that the evolution of a country's share in world trade is not always mirrored by changes in its share in world income. Indeed, while the share of industrial countries in world manufacturing trade fell over the past two decades, their share in manufacturing income rose. By contrast, the share of developing countries in both manufacturing trade and value added increased. However, this aggregate picture conceals considerable diversity in the developing world:

- First, countries that have not been able to move away from primary commodities, the markets for which are relatively stagnant or declining, have been marginalized in world trade. However, growth in trade in several primary commodities has been as rapid as in some manufactures, and countries that have successfully entered such sectors have experienced a significant expansion in their exports and incomes.

- Second, most developing countries that have been able to shift from primary commodities to manufactures have done so by focusing on resource-based, labour-intensive products which generally lack dynamism in world markets.

- Third, a number of developing countries have seen their exports rise rapidly in skill- and technology-intensive products, which have enjoyed a rapid expansion in world trade over the past two decades. However, with some notable exceptions, the involvement of developing countries in the manufacture of such products has been confined to labour-intensive, assembly-type processes with little value added. Consequently, the share of some of these countries in world manufacturing income actually fell. For others, increases in manufacturing value added lagged considerably behind their recorded shares in world manufacturing trade.

- Finally, a few economies have seen sharp increases in their shares in world manufacturing value added, which have matched or exceeded increases in their shares in world manufacturing trade. This group includes some East Asian NIEs that had already achieved considerable progress in industrialization before other developing economies began to shift their emphasis to export-oriented production. However, none of these other economies which have rapidly liberalized trade and investment in the past two decades is in this group.

With the exception of this last group, therefore, exports of developing countries continue to be concentrated on resource-based, labour-intensive products. Market growth is slow for many of these products, which continue to be protected in industrial countries. While expansion in such sectors can allow countries at the lower end of development to improve employment and income, for more advanced developing countries they offer little, since their productivity potential is limited compared to that of skill- and technology-intensive products. As discussed in the next chapter, a simultaneous drive by a large number of developing countries – especially those with large economies – to expand such exports, and increased competition among them to attract FDI for labour-intensive segments of vertically integrated production networks could be self-defeating. For many countries, rapid upgrading into market- and supply-dynamic products, combined with greater reliance on domestic markets, appears to be a more viable strategy for the expansion of industrial activity than extending the existing pattern of production and trade. In this process, technological upgrading can play a crucial role not only by enhancing the gains from trade, but also by expanding the domestic market through increases in productivity and wages. In countries located in the low-wage, labour-intensive segments of international production networks, further progress in capacity-building and industrialization calls for a strategy designed to replace imported skill- and technology-intensive parts and components with domestically produced ones in order to raise the domestic value-added content of exports. In most countries, this would require a different approach to FDI and TNCs than has hitherto been pursued.

Annex 1.A

GROWTH AND CLASSIFICATION OF WORLD MERCHANDISE EXPORTS

This annex provides basic information that underlies the analysis of export dynamism in world merchandise trade. Table 1.A1 lists 225 product categories classified in the Standard International Trade Classification (SITC), Rev. 2, at the 3-digit level. The product groups are ordered according to the average annual growth rate of their export value during the period 1980–1998, which is used as an indication of "market dynamism". The table also classifies each product group into different categories according to the mix of different skill, technology and capital intensities and scale characteristics, as follows:

Primary commodities – A
Labour-intensive and resource-based manufactures – B
Manufactures with low skill and technology intensity – C
Manufactures with medium skill and technology intensity – D
Manufactures with high skill and technology intensity – E
Unclassified products – F

A few SITC items are not considered in the analysis because data for these categories are incomplete. These items are: SITC 286 (ores and concentrates of uranium and thorium), SITC 333 (crude petroleum), SITC 351 (electric current), SITC 675 (iron and steel hoops and strips), SITC 688 (uranium and thorium), SITC 911 (postal packages), SITC 931 (special transactions and unclassified commodities), SITC 961 (coin other than gold coin), and SITC 971 (gold).

Some other items of SITC section 3, namely SITC 322 (coal), SITC 323 (coke and briquettes), SITC 334 and 335 (petroleum products), and SITC 341 (gas) are also not considered because the analysis only covers non-fuel merchandise trade.

Table 1.A2 specifies the most market-dynamic products in the exports of developed countries, developing countries as a group, and the four regional subgroups that are discussed in section E of this chapter. The product groups highlighted in the table are among the 20 most market-dynamic ones on a world scale, as listed in table 1.A1 and also in table 1.1 in the main text.

Table 1.A1

SITC PRODUCT GROUPS: AVERAGE ANNUAL GROWTH OF EXPORT VALUE, 1980–1998, AND CLASSIFICATION ACCORDING TO FACTOR INTENSITY

(Ranked by export value growth)

Rank	SITC code	Product group (SITC nomenclature)	Product category	Average annual export value growth (Per cent)
1	776	Thermionic, cold and photo-cathode valves, tubes, and parts	E	16.3
2	752	Automatic data processing machines and units thereof	E	15.0
3	759	Parts of and accessories suitable for 751, 752	E	14.6
4	871	Optical instruments and apparatus	E	14.1
5	553	Perfumery, cosmetics and toilet preparations	E	13.3
6	261	Silk	A	13.2
7	846	Undergarments, knitted or crocheted	B	13.1
8	893	Articles of materials described in division 58	D	13.1
9	771	Electric power machinery, and parts thereof	D	12.9
10	898	Musical instruments, parts and accessories	F	12.6
11	612	Manufactures of leather or of composition leather, n.e.s.	B	12.4
12	111	Non-alcoholic beverages, n.e.s.	A	12.2
13	872	Medical instruments and appliances	E	12.1
14	773	Equipment for distributing electricity	D	12.0
15	764	Telecommunications equipment, and parts	E	11.9
16	844	Undergarments of textile fabrics	B	11.9
17	048	Cereal preparations and preparations of flour or starch of fruits or vegetables	A	11.9
18	655	Knitted or crocheted fabrics	B	11.7
19	541	Medicinal and pharmaceutical products	E	11.6
20	778	Electrical machinery and apparatus, n.e.s.	D	11.5
21	873	Meters and counters, n.e.s.	E	11.3
22	514	Nitrogen-function compounds	E	11.2
23	098	Edible products and preparations, n.e.s.	A	11.2
24	772	Electrical apparatus such as switches, relays, fuses and plugs	D	11.1
25	783	Road motor vehicles, n.e.s.	D	11.1
26	821	Furniture and parts thereof	B	11.0
27	062	Sugar confectionery and other sugar preparations	A	10.9
28	592	Starches, inulin and wheat gluten, albuminoidal substances	E	10.9
29	761	Television receivers	E	10.7
30	812	Sanitary, plumbing, heating and lighting fixtures	C	10.7
31	122	Tobacco, manufactured	A	10.7
32	679	Iron and steel castings, forgings and stampings	C	10.7
33	073	Chocolate and other food preparations containing cocoa	A	10.7
34	628	Articles of rubber, n.e.s.	D	10.6
35	843	Outergarments, women's, of textile fabrics	B	10.5
36	533	Pigments, paints, varnishes and related materials	E	10.3
37	635	Wood manufactures, n.e.s.	B	10.3
38	847	Clothing accessories of textile fabrics	B	10.3
39	657	Special textile fabrics and related products	B	10.3
40	664	Glass	B	10.2
41	583	Polymerization and copolymerization products	E	10.1
42	895	Office and stationery supplies, n.e.s.	F	10.0
43	642	Paper and paperboard, cut to size or shape	B	10.0
44	621	Materials of rubber (pastes, plates, sheets)	D	9.9
45	845	Outergarments and other articles, knitted	B	9.9

46	899	Other miscellaneous manufactured articles	F	9.9
47	743	Pumps, compressors, fans and blowers	D	9.8
48	672	Ingots and other primary forms, of iron or steel	C	9.8
49	774	Electric and radiological apparatus, for medical purposes	D	9.8
50	842	Outergarments, men's, of textile fabrics	B	9.8
51	633	Cork manufactures	B	9.7
52	714	Engines and motors, non-electric	D	9.7
53	726	Printing and bookbinding machinery, and parts	D	9.7
54	551	Essential oils, perfume and flavour materials	E	9.7
55	554	Soap, cleansing and polishing preparations	E	9.7
56	611	Leather	B	9.7
57	749	Non-electric accessories of machinery	D	9.6
58	941	Animals, live, n.e.s., including zoo-animals	F	9.5
59	728	Machinery and equipment specialized for particular industries	D	9.5
60	781	Passenger motor cars, for transport of passengers and goods	D	9.4
61	515	Organo-inorganic and heterocyclic compounds	E	9.4
62	582	Condensation, polycondensation and polyaddition products	E	9.4
63	699	Manufactures of base metal, n.e.s.	C	9.4
64	598	Miscellaneous chemical products, n.e.s.	E	9.3
65	694	Nails, screws, nuts and bolts of iron, steel or copper	C	9.2
66	658	Made-up articles, wholly or chiefly of textile materials	B	9.2
67	036	Crustaceans and molluscs, fresh, chilled, frozen, salted, in brine or dried	A	9.1
68	894	Baby carriages and toys	B	9.1
69	716	Rotating electric plant and parts	D	9.1
70	775	Household type, electrical and non-electrical equipment	D	9.1
71	245	Fuel wood (excluding wood waste) and wood charcoal	A	9.0
72	034	Fish, fresh (live or dead), chilled or frozen	A	9.0
73	831	Travel goods, handbags, briefcases, purses and sheaths	B	9.0
74	713	Internal combustion piston engines, and parts	D	8.9
75	741	Heating and cooling equipment, and parts	D	8.9
76	656	Tulle, lace, embroidery, and small wares	B	8.8
77	531	Synthetic organic dyestuffs, etc., natural indigo and colour lakes	E	8.8
78	744	Mechanical handling equipment, and parts	D	8.7
79	792	Aircraft and associated equipment, and parts	E	8.7
80	784	Parts and accessories of 722, 781, 782, 783	D	8.7
81	269	Old clothing and other old textile articles; rags	A	8.7
82	874	Measuring, checking, analysing instruments	E	8.7
83	684	Aluminium	A	8.6
84	037	Fish, crustaceans and molluscs, prepared or preserved, n.e.s.	A	8.6
85	742	Pumps for liquids, liquid elevators, and parts	D	8.6
86	663	Mineral manufactures, n.e.s.	B	8.6
87	848	Articles of apparel and clothing accessories, non-textile	B	8.6
88	897	Jewellery, goldsmiths and other articles of precious materials	F	8.6
89	641	Paper and paperboard	B	8.5
90	725	Machinery for paper and pulp mills and paper manufactures	D	8.5
91	892	Printed matter	F	8.5
92	653	Fabrics, woven, of man-made fibres	B	8.5
93	634	Veneers, plywood, improved or reconstituted wood	B	8.4
94	513	Carboxylic acids, and their anhydrides, halides, and derivatives	E	8.4
95	516	Other organic chemicals	E	8.4
96	273	Stone, sand and gravel	A	8.3
97	112	Alcoholic beverages	A	8.3
98	785	Motorcycles, motor scooters and invalid carriages	C	8.3
99	512	Alcohols, phenols, phenol-alcohols, and their derivatives	E	8.2
100	665	Glassware	B	8.2

155	424	Other fixed vegetable oils, fluid or solid, crude, refined or purified	A	5.7
156	244	Cork, natural, raw and waste (including in blocks or sheets)	A	5.7
157	782	Motor vehicles for transport of goods materials	D	5.7
158	751	Office machines	E	5.6
159	693	Wire products and fencing grills	C	5.5
160	056	Vegetables, roots and tubers, prepared or preserved, n.e.s.	A	5.5
161	081	Feeding stuff for animals (not including unmilled cereals)	A	5.5
162	267	Other man-made fibres suitable for spinning and waste	A	5.4
163	721	Agricultural machinery and parts	D	5.4
164	718	Other power generating machinery and parts	D	5.3
165	572	Explosives and pyrotechnic products	E	5.2
166	562	Fertilizers, manufactured	E	5.0
167	793	Ships, boats and floating structures	C	5.0
168	035	Fish, dried, salted or in brine; smoked fish	A	4.9
169	673	Iron and steel bars, rods, angles, shapes and sections	C	4.9
170	251	Pulp and waste paper	A	4.9
171	075	Spices	A	4.8
172	001	Live animals, chiefly for food	A	4.7
173	676	Rails and railway track construction material	C	4.6
174	246	Pulpwood (including chips and wood waste)	A	4.5
175	233	Synthetic rubber latex; synthetic rubber and reclaimed rubber; waste and scrap	A	4.5
176	263	Cotton	A	4.5
177	266	Synthetic fibres suitable for spinning	A	4.4
178	211	Hides and skins (except fur skins), raw	A	4.4
179	042	Rice	A	4.4
180	511	Hydrocarbons, n.e.s., and their halogenated or derivatives	E	4.4
181	712	Steam and other vapour power units, steam engines	D	4.2
182	277	Natural abrasives, n.e.s. (including industrial diamonds)	A	4.2
183	247	Other wood in the rough or roughly squared	A	4.2
184	711	Steam and other vapour generating boilers, and parts	D	4.2
185	278	Other crude minerals	A	4.1
186	287	Ores and concentrates of base metals, n.e.s.	A	3.9
187	691	Structures and parts of structures; iron, steel and aluminium	C	3.8
188	223	Oil-seeds and oleaginous fruit, whole or broken (non-defatted flours and meals)	A	3.7
189	047	Other cereal meals and flours	A	3.6
190	025	Eggs and yolks, fresh, dried or otherwise preserved, sweetened or not	A	3.5
191	046	Meal and flour of wheat and flour of meslin	A	3.5
192	723	Civil engineering and contractors plant and parts	D	3.5
193	121	Tobacco, unmanufactured; tobacco refuse	A	3.4
194	012	Meat and edible meat offals (except poultry liver), salted, in brine, dried or smoked	A	3.2
195	678	Tubes, pipes and fittings, of iron or steel	C	3.1
196	722	Tractors fitted or not with power take-offs	D	3.0
197	222	Oil-seeds and oleaginous fruit, whole or broken (excluding flours and meals)	A	2.9
198	883	Cinematograph film, exposed and developed, negative or positive	E	2.8
199	074	Tea and maté	A	2.8
200	061	Sugar and honey	A	2.6
201	685	Lead	A	2.4
202	072	Cocoa	A	2.4
203	281	Iron ore and concentrates	A	2.4
204	584	Regenerated cellulose; cellulose nitrate and other cellulose esters	E	2.4
205	951	Armoured fighting vehicles, arms of war and ammunition	F	2.3
206	681	Silver, platinum and other metals of the platinum group	A	1.9
207	265	Vegetable textile fibres and waste of such fibres	A	1.7
208	232	Natural rubber latex; natural rubber and similar natural gums	A	1.6
209	524	Radioactive and associated materials	E	1.5

Source: UNCTAD secretariat calculations, based on UN/DESA, Commodity Trade Statistics database.

Table 1.A2

LEADING MARKET-DYNAMIC PRODUCTS BY EXPORTING REGION,
RANKED BY AVERAGE ANNUAL EXPORT VALUE GROWTH, 1980–1998

Rank	SITC code	Product group	Rank	SITC code	Product group
		Developed countries			*Developing countries*
1	776	Transistors and semiconductors	1	752	Computers
2	844	Textile undergarments	2	871	Optical instruments
3	553	Perfumery and cosmetics	3	759	Parts of computers and office machines
4	871	Optical instruments	4	582	Condensation products
5	752	Computers	5	741	Heating and cooling equipment, and parts
6	893	Plastic articles	6	655	Knitted fabrics
7	759	Parts of computers and office machines	7	531	Synthetic organic dyestuffs
8	898	Musical instruments and records	8	773	Electricity distribution equipment
9	541	Pharmaceutical products	9	712	Steam engines and turbines
10	846	Knitted undergarments	10	781	Passenger motor vehicles
11	872	Medical instruments	11	872	Medical instruments
12	048	Cereal preparations	12	763	Sound recorders
13	111	Non-alcoholic beverages	13	583	Polymerization products
14	764	Telecom equipment, and parts	14	776	Transistors and semiconductors
15	771	Electric power machinery	15	771	Electric power machinery
16	783	Buses and tractors	16	679	Iron and steel castings
17	098	Preserved food	17	774	Medical apparatus
18	514	Nitrogen-function compounds	18	592	Starch, inulin, gluten, albuminoidal substances
19	873	Meters and counters	19	516	Other organic chemicals
20	073	Chocolate	20	761	Television sets
		First-tier NIEs			*ASEAN-4*
1	752	Computers	1	752	Computers
2	277	Natural abrasives	2	759	Parts of computers and office machines
3	783	Buses and tractors	3	871	Optical instruments
4	951	War firearms and ammunition	4	763	Sound recorders
5	871	Optical instruments	5	672	Iron or steel ingots and forms
6	592	Starch, inulin, gluten, albuminoidal substances	6	751	Office machines
7	781	Passenger motor vehicles	7	716	Rotating electric plant and parts
8	611	Leather	8	511	Hydrocarbons
9	212	Raw furskins	9	277	Natural abrasives
10	582	Condensation products	10	761	Television sets
11	882	Photographic and cinematographic supplies	11	785	Cycles and motor cycles
12	682	Copper	12	773	Electricity distribution equipment
13	759	Parts of computers and office machines	13	267	Other man-made fibres

14	686	Zinc	14	786	Non-motor vehicles
15	513	Carboxylic acids	15	775	Household equipment
16	524	Radioactive materials	16	641	Paper and paperboard
17	122	Manufactured tobacco	17	592	Starch, inulin, gluten, albuminoidal substances
18	712	Steam engines and turbines	18	677	Iron or steel wire
19	774	Medical apparatus	19	781	Passenger motor vehicles
20	515	Organo-inorganic compounds	20	268	Wool and animal hair

	South Asia			**South America**	
1	761	Television sets	1	245	Fuel wood and charcoal
2	752	**Computers**	2	682	Copper
3	582	Condensation products	3	292	Crude vegetable materials
4	674	Iron or steel universals, plates and sheets	4	098	Preserved food
5	515	Organo-inorganic compounds	5	014	Meat preparations
6	655	**Knitted fabrics**	6	121	Unmanufactured tobacco
7	266	Synthetic fibres for spinning	7	524	Radioactive materials
8	672	Iron or steel ingots and forms	8	716	Rotating electric plant and parts
9	871	**Optical instruments**	9	678	Iron or steel tubes, pipes and fittings
10	759	**Parts of computers and office machines**	10	812	Plumbing, heating, and lighting equipment
11	673	Iron and steel bars and rods	11	523	Other inorganic chemicals
12	513	Carboxylic acids	12	111	**Non-alcoholic beverages**
13	661	Lime, cement and building products	13	845	Knitted outergarments
14	583	Polymerization products	14	951	War firearms and ammunition
15	514	Nitrogen-function compounds	15	713	Internal combustion piston engines and parts
16	277	Natural abrasives	16	045	Unmilled cereals
17	511	Hydrocarbons	17	671	Pig iron
18	683	Nickel	18	046	Wheat meal or flour
19	898	Musical instruments and records	19	551	Essential oils, perfume and flavour materials
20	781	Passenger motor vehicles	20	655	**Knitted fabrics**

Source: See table 1.A1.

Note: The product groups highlighted are among the 20 most market-dynamic ones on a world scale, as listed in table 1.A1 of this annex and table 1.1 in the main text.

Annex 1.B

UNITED STATES TRADE
PRICES AND DYNAMIC PRODUCTS

This annex uses the data available on United States export and import prices to assess the extent to which the results reported in section B on dynamic products change when exports are measured at constant prices. The United States Bureau of Labor Statistics (BLS) began developing and publishing annual indices for import and export prices for United States merchandise and services trade in 1989 (monthly indices have been published since January 1993). In preparing these, the BLS has tried to ensure that the prices used refer to products of unchanged quality in terms of technical specification. Where there are significant changes in specification, an adjustment is made to ensure that "the index reflects only actual or 'pure' price changes and is not moved by quality changes" (BLS, 1997: 156).

Chart 1.B1 shows the evolution of United States export and import price indices for four of the most dynamic products in world markets (see section B and annex A).[26] Of these, import prices of both computers, and parts of computers and office machines have been more volatile than their export prices, and they showed a steep decline during the period 1995–1998. Similarly, for telecommunications equipment, the import price index declined between 1981 and 1985, recovered sharply in subsequent years, and again fell at a steeper rate than export prices after 1995. For such items as transistors and semiconductors, import and export price indices moved more or less together on a downward trend until 1995, but thereafter the import price index fell considerably more sharply than the export price index.

An examination of United States trade statistics suggests that the export price index can be taken as a proxy for prices in trade among developed countries, and the import price index as a proxy for developing countries' export prices. In 1998, in value terms, developing countries accounted for about two thirds of total United States imports of computers, parts of computers and office machines, and transistors and semiconductors, and for about 60 per cent of United States imports of telecommunications equipment. Two thirds of total United States

---

[26] The indices are annual data obtained by averaging BLS's monthly or quarterly data, depending on data availability.

Chart 1.B1

**UNITED STATES IMPORT AND EXPORT PRICE INDICES FOR SELECTED
ELECTRONICS PRODUCTS, 1980-2000**

(Index numbers, 1995 = 100)

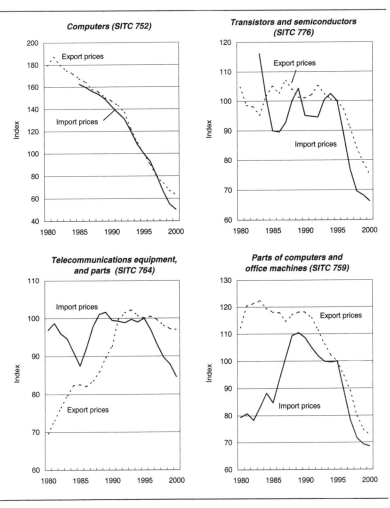

Source: UNCTAD secretariat calculations, based on data from the United States Department of Labor (www.bis.gov/datahome.htm).

computer exports and exports of parts of computers and office machines went to developed countries, which were also the destination for about half of all United States exports of telecommunications equipment, and one fourth of its exports of transistors and semiconductors; of the latter products, over 70 per cent went to developing countries. Using the United States import prices as a proxy, the evidence presented in chart 1.B1 suggests that developing country export prices for the four dynamic products have been subject to a higher degree of volatility over the past two decades, and that they also experienced steeper falls after 1995 than the export and import prices of the same products traded among developed countries.

The BLS data do not allow for a comprehensive estimation of export growth in constant prices. The available data show that there have been sharp declines in both export and import prices of computers and office equipment (SITC 75). The steepest decline in this product division was in the import price index of computers, which steadily fell from 163 in 1985 to 50 in 2000. Prices of telecommunications, audio and video equipment (SITC 76), and electrical machinery and appliances (SITC 77) also declined. However, the decline was only in their import price index and it was relatively moderate (from 106 in 1980 to 84 in 2000 for the former, and from 85 in 1981 to 83 in 2000 for the latter).[27] Within the latter division, it declined the most for transistors and semiconductors (from 116 in 1983 to 66 in 2000). The strongest fall in the import price index after 1995 was recorded for computers, followed by transistors and semiconductors.

These observations suggest that the rate of export growth in computers, parts of computers and office machines, and transistors and semiconductors would dwarf export growth in other products if exports could be expressed in terms of constant prices. On the other hand, they

---

[27] Tropical beverages is the only other product item at the 2-digit SITC level in the BLS import price database for which the index value in 1980 was higher than in 2000 (98 in 1980 compared to 58 in 2000).

also show that the ranking of products reported in section B would not change significantly.

Annex 1.C

INTERNATIONAL PRODUCTION NETWORKS AND INDUSTRIALIZATION IN DEVELOPING COUNTRIES

This annex examines how international production sharing has influenced the process of industrialization and growth in developing countries. It concentrates on three sectors that have been important in international production networks involving developing countries in recent years. These sectors, however, differ in the way they operate: the clothing sector is based on subcontracting, the electronics sector is governed by TNCs, and the automobile sector is strongly influenced by preferential trade agreements.

1. Outsourcing: the clothing sector

While FDI has played some role, the major form of production relocation in the clothing sector has been outsourcing.[28] Compared to traditional arm's-length transactions, outsourcing entails greater stability in business relationships and better provision of information in the form of detailed instructions and specifications. The leading actors in such inter-firm networks, based on a contractual relationship, are large retailers of standardized products and brand-name merchandisers of private label products. While the former tend to rely on global production networks based on agreements to purchase the final product from a local producer (full package subcontracting), the latter tend to create regional production networks, where the leading firm delivers semi-finished products to a subcontractor and buys back the finished product (assembly subcontracting).

Industrialization in many developing countries has focused on textiles and clothing. As a labour-intensive sector, clothing provides significant job opportunities in labour-abundant economies which have a comparative advantage due to lower wages. Moreover, for over 20 years the quota regulations of the Multi-Fibre Arrangement (MFA) have enabled latecomers to access markets for clothing and textiles once competing countries have filled their MFA quotas. More recently, improvements in production and communication technologies and falling transport costs have enabled geographical separation of the labour-

---

[28] On the role of FDI in this context, see Mortimore, Lall and Romijn (2000); on outsourcing, see Graziani (2001) and Gereffi (1999).

intensive segments from the skill- and capital-intensive segments of the manufacturing process in textiles and clothing. For example, while growing automation has increased the capital-intensity of the pre-assembling stages of the production process, the assembling stages have remained relatively labour-intensive. As a result, it has become both technically feasible and economically profitable for high-wage country manufacturers to relocate their assembling stages of production to low-wage countries and to re-import the end products for domestic sale or for export to third markets.

The benefits of international production sharing in clothing for technology transfer and industrialization in developing countries have been uneven. They vary, in particular, according to whether outsourcing involves full-package agreements or simple assembly subcontracting. For example, the East Asian economies have gone through a sequence, from assembly to full-package operations and, in some cases, to original brand manufacturing; in Mexico there has been an ongoing transition from assembly to a more full-package type of production, favoured by regulations under the North American Free Trade Agreement (NAFTA); and the Caribbean countries have continued to perform labour-intensive assembly operations that generate few benefits for their local economies, except low-wage employment (ECLAC, 1999).

The first-tier NIEs in East Asia were the first to establish production facilities under outsourcing agreements with large United States retailers and brand-name merchandisers. Local producers conducted simple assembly activities for a short period of time before moving rapidly to a system of brand-name subcontracting, whereby they produced according to designs specified by the buyer. Many firms proceeded further to original brand-name manufacturing. This was facilitated by a number of factors, including the specialization of East Asian exporters in a wide array of fabrics favoured by women's wear branded marketers, and the geographical distance from the United States which made the use of United States textiles impractical. As trade regulations in destination markets became increasingly restrictive, and rising costs and appreciating exchange rates began to constrain the competitiveness of local producers, many firms in the first-tier NIEs started to concentrate on skill-intensive activities and to outsource the labour-intensive operations of clothing production to their lesser developed neighbours where wages were lower. Social and cultural factors (such as a common language) appear to have been important in their choice of countries for relocation.

Outsourcing, together with the quota advantages of the new assembly sites, has given rise to a triangular manufacturing system, whereby firms of the first-tier NIEs export directly to the United States from their lower-wage sites in neighbouring countries. Thus the first-tier NIEs have sustained their involvement in world trade in textiles and clothing through industrial upgrading: from cheap standardized goods to expensive differentiated goods, from simple assembly of imported inputs to integrated forms of production with greater forward and backward linkages, and from bilateral interregional trade flows to a more fully developed intraregional division of labour incorporating all phases of production and marketing. However, since triangular manufacturing involves considerable coordination costs, without further industrial upgrading the first-tier NIEs may face increased competition from those less advanced Asian countries that have the potential to upgrade from assembling to full-package manufacturing.

The East Asian experience in outsourcing contrasts sharply with that of Mexico and the Caribbean countries. The participation of the latter countries in international production sharing was stimulated by the stiff competition that United States brand-name manufacturers faced from Asian producers. They provided attractive locations because of low wages, which continues to be a key factor in their participation in production sharing in clothing. Furthermore, they benefit from preferential market access provided under Chapter 98 of the Harmonized Tariff Schedule of the United States. However, Mexico has a greater advantage owing to the rules of origin of NAFTA, whereby its inputs into goods for export count as North American inputs and, therefore, are not taxed at the United States border. Caribbean countries, on the other hand, operate under the United States production sharing mechanism, which, while offering privileged access to the United States market, taxes non-United States inputs. The incorporation of competitive Mexican inputs into final products destined for export markets (USITC, 1999b: 30) provides an opportunity to deepen integration, but this will depend on the evolution of competitiveness of the Mexican textiles industry. By contrast, producers in the Caribbean countries have not progressed beyond simple assembly-type processes. After the phasing out of the Agreement on Textiles and Clothing (ATC) of the WTO, they are likely to face strong competition from exporters in South Asia and China, which may lead to a race to the bottom in wage cuts and other incentives needed to attract outsourcing contracts.

Table 1.C1

**BILATERAL TRADE IN APPAREL AND CLOTHING ACCESSORIES
BETWEEN SELECTED TRADING PARTNERS, 1980–1998**

(Percentage shares in total world exports)

	1980	1985	1990	1995	1998
Exports of EU-8 to:					
EU-8	26.2	17.0	17.5	13.1	12.4
European periphery	1.5	1.1	2.3	2.3	2.4
Eastern Europe	0.3	0.2	0.3	1.0	1.1
First-tier NIEs	0.3	0.3	0.7	1.1	0.6
ASEAN-4	0.0	0.0	0.0	0.0	0.0
China	0.0	0.0	0.0	0.0	0.0
North Africa	0.3	0.2	0.3	0.4	0.5
Imports of EU-8 from:					
European periphery	3.3	5.4	6.8	6.2	5.6
Eastern Europe	0.8	0.5	0.7	4.2	4.6
First-tier NIEs	9.3	5.2	4.8	2.6	2.0
ASEAN-4	1.0	0.7	1.9	1.7	1.3
China	0.0	0.6	0.9	1.5	1.5
North Africa	1.3	1.0	1.8	2.0	1.9
Exports of United States to:					
First-tier NIEs	0.1	0.0	0.0	0.1	0.0
ASEAN-4	0.0	0.0	0.0	0.0	0.0
China	0.0	0.0	0.0	0.0	0.0
Mexico	0.5	0.4	0.4	0.9	1.5
Caribbean	0.7	0.6	0.8	1.7	2.2
Imports of United States from:					
First-tier NIEs	11.8	17.9	10.9	6.2	5.6
ASEAN-4	0.5	1.8	2.1	2.8	3.6
China	0.0	1.2	1.1	2.1	2.2
Mexico	0.0	0.5	0.1	1.8	3.8
Caribbean	0.0	0.8	0.2	0.7	0.6
Exports of Japan to:					
First-tier NIEs	0.1	0.2	0.1	0.1	0.1
ASEAN-4	0.0	0.0	0.0	0.0	0.0
China	0.0	0.0	0.0	0.1	0.0
Imports of Japan from:					
First-tier NIEs	2.2	2.4	3.4	1.7	0.7
ASEAN-4	0.1	0.0	0.4	0.7	0.4
China	0.0	0.8	1.3	5.0	4.4
Exports of first-tier NIEs to:					
China	0.0	0.1	0.3	0.6	1.2
Imports of first-tier NIEs from:					
China	0.0	0.6	4.7	4.9	6.1

Source: UNCTAD secretariat calculations, based on UN/DESA, *Commodity Trade Statistics* database.

Note: Data in this table relates to SITC 84. The composition of the regional/subregional groups is as follows:

EU-8: Belgium, Denmark, France, Germany, Italy, Luxembourg, the Netherlands, United Kingdom.

European periphery: Greece, Ireland, Portugal, Spain, Turkey.

Eastern Europe: Bulgaria, Czech Republic (1995 and 1998), Czechoslovakia (1980–1990), Estonia (1995 and 1998), Hungary, Latvia (1995 and 1998), Lithuania (1995 and 1998), Poland, Romania, Slovakia (1995 and 1998), Slovenia.

Caribbean: Antigua and Barbuda, Aruba, Bahamas, Barbados, Belize, British Virgin Islands, Costa Rica, Dominica, Dominican Republic, El Salvador, Grenada, Guatemala, Guyana, Haiti, Honduras, Jamaica, Montserrat, Netherlands Antilles, Nicaragua, Panama, St Kitts and Nevis, Saint Lucia, Saint Vincent and the Grenadines, Trinidad and Tobago.

First-tier NIEs: Hong Kong (China), Republic of Korea, Singapore, Taiwan Province of China.

ASEAN-4: Indonesia, Malaysia, the Philippines, Thailand.

North Africa: Egypt, Morocco, Tunisia.

The outsourcing agreements have had a strong impact on the direction of trade in clothing. The evidence presented in table 1.C1 indicates a sizeable increase in two-way trade between the core countries of the EU (EU-8) and their neighbouring regions at different levels of per capita income (European periphery, Eastern Europe and North Africa), on the one hand, and that between the United States and Mexico and the Caribbean countries, on the other. In all these cases, except for the bilateral trade between the United States and the Caribbean countries, the increase in exports from poorer to richer countries exceeds that of the reverse trade flows. There was a sharp decline in apparel imports by the United States and the EU-8 (and later also by Japan) from the first-tier NIEs, accompanied by a sharp increase in their imports from the ASEAN-4 and, in particular, China. There is also a sizeable increase in two-way trade between the first-tier NIEs and China. These findings document both the tendency towards regionalization in the clothing trade and the emergence of triangular manufacturing centred on the first-tier NIEs.

2. *Production networks driven by TNCs: the electronics industry*

The electronics industry is arguably the most globalized of all industries. Trade in electronics products is underpinned by an increasing geographic dispersion of TNC-driven production networks. Developing economies, notably in East Asia, have been playing a growing role in such networks, and electronics products now account for a significant proportion of their exports. They therefore provide an interesting case to assess the scope for industrial upgrading in the context of international production networks.

The electronics industry is the single most important sector for investment by both Japanese and United States TNCs in East Asia; during the early 1990s it accounted for about 45 per cent of the total manufacturing FDI of Japan and 25 per cent of that of the United States (Ernst and Ravenhill, 1999:36). United States producers of semiconductors and computer equipment started to invest in export-oriented, labour-intensive assembly production in East Asia in the late 1960s, taking advantage of the low cost of labour there. Subsequently, United States producers and mass merchandisers of household appliances started to outsource an increasing variety of such products to independent suppliers in East Asia. As discussed in detail in *TDR 1996*, export-oriented Japanese TNCs began to shift their production bases offshore in the mid-1980s as they came under heavy pressure from a rising yen and increased protectionist tendencies in other major industrialized countries.

The East Asian countries offered attractive locations because of their relatively low labour costs, high levels of education and skills, and good physical infrastructure, and because exports from these countries did not face the same increase in protectionist barriers as exports from Japan.

Even though there is little detailed comparative empirical evidence, there appear to be significant differences in the way Japanese and United States TNCs organize their production networks in East Asia, particularly with regard to the location of management, the sourcing of components and capital goods, the replication of production networks, and the motive for investing abroad (Belderbos, Capannelli and Fukao, 2001; Ernst and Ravenhill, 1999).

The traditional Japanese corporate management system relies much more on intra-firm cooperative arrangements within vertically integrated conglomerates (*keiretsu*) than the United States management system, which relies on market-based relationships with relatively more independent affiliates. Consequently, Japanese affiliates are less likely to employ local managers or local personnel in senior technical tasks than their United States counterparts. For the same reason, Japanese companies are also more reluctant to transfer research and development (R&D) activities to overseas subsidiaries. High coordination costs and slow interaction between producers and customers are major drawbacks of the Japanese system. However, initially these did not present serious problems, since Japanese investment in East Asia concentrated on lower-end consumer electronics (such as television sets and household appliances) and related standardized components that do not require close interaction with customers yet allow significant benefits from scale economies. Investments of United States TNCs, by contrast, have concentrated on integrated circuits and products related to personal computers (PCs) that are highly differentiated and thus require close interaction with customers. However, following the liberalization of the Japanese computer market and the shift by many Japanese companies from mainframe to PC-based systems in the early 1990s, Japanese affiliates in East Asia have increasingly moved towards producing PC-related products as well.

Until recently, affiliates of Japanese TNCs were less inclined to establish backward linkages with domestic firms in the host countries than affiliates of United States TNCs, tending to rely more on imports of components and materials from Japan. This was partly because of their more hierarchical and centralized management structure. Japanese FDI in the export-oriented electronics sector also started much later than FDI from the United States. Since it takes time to establish relationships with local suppliers who can meet international standards in price, quality, design and delivery, Japanese affiliates tended to procure components from secure and reliable suppliers in Japan. The Japanese suppliers were also able to provide components conforming to specialized in-house designs that were preferred over the local suppliers' standard designs. However, since the early 1990s, as a result of growing price competition from United States companies in electronic data processing equipment, Japanese producers increased their purchases of end-products in East Asia and shifted part of their production to that region (Ernst and Guerrieri, 1998: 201).

Differences in the motives for investment abroad have also resulted in different practices. While United States TNCs have traditionally sought lower-cost production sites, the motive of Japanese investors has often been to jump trade barriers against Japanese exports, such as voluntary export restraints (VERs) or anti-dumping practices. One consequence of this has been the development of a triangular trade pattern, whereby Japanese affiliates source components from Japan and export the final products directly from their offshore sites to third markets.

The traditional intra-firm pattern continues to govern the activities of Japanese TNCs in consumer electronics and appliances, but there are indications that Japanese affiliates involved in computer-related products are increasingly moving towards more local sourcing of components and materials, and are becoming more embedded in the host economies. One reason is the development of local production capabilities in host countries. Another is the increasing need to use cheaper mass-produced components as a result of tougher competition, and the growing importance of speed-to-market (i.e. getting the right product to the most buoyant markets on time), for which the traditional Japanese management system was ill-equipped.

These developments have resulted in the emergence of a pattern of regional specialization in East Asia that encompasses both parent-affiliate and inter-firm supplier networks. Of these, the latter is becoming more important, as firms increasingly focus on core competencies and purchase intermediate goods and services from other firms. Although details differ for different product groups, both United States and Japanese firms have concentrated on the same types of activities in the same economies: Hong Kong (China) and Singapore compete for regional headquarters; the

Republic of Korea and Taiwan Province of China compete for original equipment manufacturer contracts and as suppliers of precision instruments; Malaysia, the Philippines and Thailand compete as locations for mid-level and some higher-tech products that involve scale economies; and China and Indonesia (and, to some extent, Viet Nam) compete for low-end and simple component manufacturing.[29]

The evolution of the electronics industry in East Asia differs across countries. The experience of the Republic of Korea is of particular interest because of its success in becoming the second largest supplier, behind Japan, for a broad range of consumer electronics (audio equipment, television sets, video recorders and microwave ovens), and an increasingly significant supplier of high-precision components and industrial electronics. Despite this, the evolution of the electronics industry in the Republic of Korea has been described as "truncated industrial upgrading" in the sense that its firms have failed to upgrade certain features necessary for long-term growth and sustained industrial upgrading (Ernst, 1998). Its electronics sector consists of a few large firms that pursue a strategy of massive investment in integrated production systems; they rely on a high degree of vertical and horizontal integration, and focus on quantitative targets in capacity expansion and international market share for relatively homogeneous products such as consumer electronics and computer memories. This strategy has resulted in the development of operational capabilities in production and investment; but there is a high degree of dependence on imports of equipment and materials, and there has been little progress in knowledge upgrading in product design, market development and the provision of high-end knowledge-intensive support services.

The experience of the Republic of Korea shares certain features with the ASEAN countries and China in the way integration into international production networks has shaped the structure of their electronics sector. Specialization in standardized mass products with important scale economies tends to lead to a shallow involvement in a particular sector of the electronics industry and increases the import dependence of production. Moreover, it provides little impulse for broadening the knowledge base of the labour force. However, the Korean experience differs significantly from the more recent involvement of the ASEAN

---

[29] See Ernst (1997). Anecdotal evidence on geographical relocation of specific operational units of TNCs suggests that China has recently succeeded in upgrading its involvement in international production sharing, performing activities that are technologically and managerially more demanding (see chapter 3).

countries and China in international production sharing in electronics. With Japanese firms shifting from consumer electronics and appliances to PC-related products alongside the United States TNCs, a new pattern of regional production sharing has emerged, giving rise to overlapping and competing international production networks. This development has broadened the options available to the East Asian economies, allowing them to supply buyers in different production networks in an effort to amortize their substantial investment outlays and gain economies of scale as quickly as possible. However, it also implies that buyers have a wider choice of suppliers and will seek the best offer, in particular with respect to low-end and large-volume products. The fact that production costs of such products often depend on the length of production runs, creates a risk of overproduction and intense price competition. This risk has become particularly acute with the recent decline in world demand for products such as semiconductors.

Widening production networks in electronics have also made a significant impact on bilateral trade flows in these products. Figures on trade in parts of computers and office machines show a rapidly growing one-way trade from the first-tier NIEs and ASEAN-4 to the United States and the EU-8 (table 1.C2). This has been accompanied by a decline in Japanese exports to these destinations, and a sizeable increase in two-way bilateral trade between Japan and the first-tier NIEs and the ASEAN-4, as well as between the first-tier NIEs and the ASEAN-4. More recently, China has also become part of this pattern. These results suggest that the relocation of production from Japan to the East Asian developing countries and the creation of international production sharing among the latter have been important factors in the rapid expansion of trade in electronics products. A similar pattern of two-way bilateral trade has also evolved since the mid-1990s between the EU-8 and Eastern Europe, as well as between the United States and Mexico.

3. The effects of preferential trading arrangements: the automotive sector

Automobile production is one of the most important industrial activities in the world, and one of the fastest growing sectors in world trade. It has also played a critical role in the industrialization of many countries, including some of the larger developing countries, where its expansion has often been closely associated with an import substitution strategy. However, many developing countries have failed to establish

Table 1.C2

**BILATERAL TRADE IN PARTS OF COMPUTERS AND OFFICE MACHINES
BETWEEN SELECTED TRADING PARTNERS, 1980–1998**

(Percentage shares in total world exports)

	1980	1985	1990	1995	1998
Exports of first-tier NIEs to:					
ASEAN-4	0.1	0.4	1.4	2.1	2.0
China	0.1	0.6	0.3	0.6	0.8
Japan	0.4	0.5	0.6	1.3	1.3
EU-8	0.4	1.0	2.6	3.8	4.5
United States	4.2	4.2	4.8	7.7	5.6
Imports of first-tier NIEs from:					
ASEAN-4	0.0	0.1	2.0	3.2	3.9
China	0.0	0.0	0.2	0.9	1.2
Japan	0.8	1.0	1.7	2.9	2.0
EU-8	0.4	0.3	0.4	0.5	0.5
United States	3.4	3.8	2.2	2.1	1.8
Exports of ASEAN-4 to:					
China	0.0	0.0	0.0	0.0	0.6
Japan	0.0	0.0	0.3	0.8	1.2
EU-8	0.0	0.0	0.3	1.0	2.1
United States	0.0	0.2	0.9	2.1	3.4
Imports of ASEAN-4 from:					
China	0.0	0.0	0.0	0.0	0.2
Japan	0.1	0.1	0.5	1.0	1.2
EU-8	0.1	0.1	0.1	0.1	0.1
United States	0.1	0.3	0.3	0.7	0.6
Exports of China to:					
Japan	0.0	0.0	0.0	0.2	0.4
EU-8	0.0	0.0	0.0	0.3	0.4
United States	0.0	0.0	0.0	0.4	0.7
Imports of China from:					
Japan	0.0	0.1	0.0	0.6	0.6
EU-8	0.1	0.0	0.0	0.0	0.0
United States	0.1	0.2	0.0	0.1	0.3
Exports of EU-8 to:					
Japan	0.7	0.2	0.3	0.6	0.2
Eastern Europe	0.5	0.1	0.2	0.5	1.0
EU-8	25.7	22.9	20.5	11.7	10.0
Imports of EU-8 from:					
Japan	1.5	2.4	4.8	4.5	3.2
Eastern Europe	0.0	0.0	0.0	0.1	0.8
Exports of United States to:					
Japan	2.9	3.0	3.0	1.9	1.6
Mexico	1.7	1.6	0.9	0.8	1.3
Imports of United States from:					
Japan	2.5	5.5	9.8	8.0	5.4
Mexico	0.0	1.1	0.2	0.7	1.7

Source: See table 1.C1.
Note: Data in this table relates to SITC 759. The composition of the regional/subregional groups is as in table 1.C1.

competitive national automobile firms, in large part because the size of their domestic markets has not allowed exploitation of important scale economies that characterize this sector.

One way of overcoming this problem has been to create a regionally integrated automobile industry, supported by a preferential trade arrangement to protect it against competition from mature industries in developed economies. Indeed, one of the first consequences of regional integration in the Southern Common Market (MERCOSUR) and in the ASEAN Free Trade Area (AFTA) was the creation of regional production networks in the automobile industry and the dispersion of its manufacturing processes across national frontiers.[30] By contrast, the creation of the North American Free Trade Area (NAFTA) in 1993, as a formal regional economic arrangement between developed and developing countries, marked the culmination of existing and increasingly close trade and investment ties in specific industries, notably the automotive sector in the United States and Mexico. The following section examines the impact of MERCOSUR and AFTA on the regional pattern of trade in greater detail. This is followed by a study of the impact of NAFTA on the development of the automobile industry in Mexico.

a)   Production and trade patterns of MERCOSUR and AFTA

The evolution of the automotive sector in MERCOSUR and AFTA has been influenced not only by regional preferential trade agreements (PTAs), but also by increased activities of TNCs from the United States, Japan and the EU in these regions following their liberalization of FDI. In both regions, the removal of intraregional trade barriers increased the size of the market for firms established in the member countries, thereby allowing important scale economies. This factor, together with higher tariffs applied to imports from non-members, played an important role in attracting FDI, particularly in AFTA, where national automotive industries in Indonesia and Malaysia enjoyed a significant degree of protection against non-members. However, the pattern of integration has been somewhat different between the two regions. In AFTA, large differences in per capita incomes and labour costs of the member

---

[30] This contrasts with the traditional path of regional integration, which often involves the liberalization of trade in goods in the early stages, followed by liberalization of trade in services and of movements of labour and capital, and by increasing coordination of regulatory and other policies. A change in industry structure generally is not envisaged early in the process. For a general discussion of AFTA and MERCOSUR, see Athukorala and Menon (1997), and Preusse (2001); for a study of the automobile sector in the two regions, see Romijn, Van Assouw and Mortimore (2000).

countries have encouraged the creation of cross-border production networks within the automotive industry. By contrast, in MERCOSUR, where such differences are much smaller, investment has been driven by considerations of market size.

Intraregional trade in both automobiles and their parts and components has grown considerably in both regions, substantially exceeding their growth in world trade (table 1.C3). In MERCOSUR, imports from non-members grew substantially during the period 1990–1999, although somewhat less than imports from member countries. In AFTA, on the other hand, imports from non-members were lower in 1999 than they had been at the start of the decade, mainly as a result of the Asian financial crisis in 1997. Prior to the crisis, imports from non-members had grown fairly rapidly between 1990 and 1996 (at an average annual rate of 9.4 per cent for road vehicles and at 7.2 per cent for their parts and components, compared to growth rates in world imports of 4.5 per cent and 5.1 per cent respectively). However, on the whole, imports from non-members have been much lower in AFTA than in MERCOSUR, which reflects efforts to develop national industries in the Asian region.

Argentina and Brazil began developing automobile industries for their highly protected domestic markets in the 1950s. Since the early 1990s, the industry has undergone substantial restructuring as a result of special provisions in MERCOSUR designed to facilitate the expansion of activities of existing TNCs as well as to attract new ones. In addition, a bilateral agreement between Argentina and Brazil allows vehicles and parts to be imported duty-free, provided that the importer balances foreign purchases with exports (Romijn, Van Assouw and Mortimore, 2000: 130). These initiatives have led to the rationalization of investment and production, resulting in increased specialization and production complementarity which involved the location of the small-scale production of larger vehicles in Argentina and the large-scale production of smaller vehicles for the mass market in Brazil. The initiatives have also boosted bilateral trade. In particular, they have provided an important stimulus to Argentina's automobile industry by significantly widening its market.[31] Unlike Argentina, scale economies are more important to the

---

[31] This has also been helped by an agreement among industry, the Government and trade unions, called the "Argentine Automobile Regime", which carries an obligation to export a value approximately equal to the value of the imported components and finished vehicles (Miozzo, 2000).

Table 1.C3

**INTRAREGIONAL IMPORTS OF THE AUTOMOBILE INDUSTRY:
MERCOSUR AND AFTA, 1980–1999**

| | | Share in total imports | | | Growth rate | | *Memo item:*
Growth rate in
extraregional imports | |
| | *$ million* | | | | *(Per cent)* | | | |
Region	*1999*	*1990*	*1995*	*1999*	*1980–* *1989*	*1990–* *1999*	*1980–* *1989*	*1990–* *1999*
MERCOSUR								
Motor vehicles	2 027	41.0	19.5	52.7	15.5	40.2	-17.5	33.0
Parts of motor vehicles	694	22.6	41.8	25.1	8.9	20.8	10.4	19.0
AFTA								
Motor vehicles	175	1.1	1.0	5.4	9.4	18.6	1.5	-0.7
Parts of motor vehicles	195	1.1	2.9	9.5	17.3	20.8	14.2	-5.6
Memo item:								
WORLD								
Motor vehicles	365 672	.	.	.	10.7	6.6	.	.
Parts of motor vehicles	138 406	.	.	.	10.2	6.4	.	.

Source: See table 1.C1.
Note: Data in this table relates to SITC 781, 782, and 783 (motor vehicles), and to SITC 784 (parts of motor vehicles).

automobile industry in Brazil. For the latter country, however, regional integration has not generated much opportunity for the expansion of capacity needed to exploit scale economies. Consequently, Brazilian production has remained constrained, and low productivity associated with suboptimal production has limited exports to third markets.

National suppliers have lost importance in Brazil since 1990, when the market was opened to imports and assemblers moved increasingly towards global sourcing. Some of the transnational vehicle makers also established their own engine and component production sites; this led to the emergence of a more vertical supply structure whereby the surviving national suppliers were relegated from first- to second- or third-tier status. Argentina's auto parts industry has undergone a similar development: increased integration into international production networks has led most TNCs to concentrate design, engineering and R&D functions at headquarters, while their affiliates concentrate on manufacturing.

Indonesia, Malaysia, the Philippines and Thailand all began assembling automobiles in the late 1950s and early 1960s under relatively protective import-substitution regimes. While the industry in South America faced serious difficulties in the 1980s because of the debt crisis, in South-East Asia it entered a new phase of take-off after the mid-1980s as a result of rapid economic growth, the appreciation of the yen and the conclusion of regional trade agreements.[32] The impact of the appreciation of the yen on this industry in members of ASEAN was broadly the same as its impact on the electronics industry discussed above. Since Japanese TNCs wanted to use Japanese suppliers for their production networks, they persuaded their suppliers to establish plants in ASEAN countries (mainly Thailand). ASEAN governments adopted preferential agreements such as the ASEAN Industrial Cooperation Scheme (started in 1996), which granted some privileges – notably preferential tariffs to companies operating in an ASEAN member country and having a minimum of 30 per cent national equity – in order to help establish a more efficient regional division of labour and strengthen the competitiveness of the automobile industry.

b)   NAFTA and the Mexican automotive industry

The take-off of the Mexican automobile industry preceded NAFTA, although the latter has given it a new momentum. The sector had been established in the 1960s in the context of import substituting industrialization, in which large foreign vehicle assemblers coexisted uneasily with smaller domestic component producers under tight government regulation and supervision. Despite high tariff barriers, the sector, which was heavily dependent on imported parts but had minimal export capacity, was a constant drain on foreign exchange. It thus became unviable after the debt crisis of the early 1980s. Some tentative steps towards greater export orientation were taken in the early 1980s. However, it was the combination of the debt crisis in Mexico and a concerted effort by United States auto manufacturers to defend profits and regain market share, in response to the successful penetration of North American markets by Japanese producers, that transformed the Mexican industry. Pressure to cut costs so as to compete with the Japanese producers made Mexico an attractive location for sourcing parts, and for vehicle assembly of certain models. A policy shift in Mexico towards more liberal trade and investment regimes led to a lowering of national

---

[32] In Malaysia this take-off was additionally supported by the launch of a "national car" project in 1983.

content requirements for exported products (permitting 70 per cent of imported components for exports compared to 40 per cent for sales in the domestic market). Along with specific incentives offered by both the United States and Mexican authorities to attract foreign producers into the automotive sector, this shift generated a burst of FDI in the Mexican automobile industry, beginning in the mid-1980s and accelerating in the first half of the 1990s (Romijn, Van Assouw and Mortimore, 2000).

Renewed TNC activity in Mexico led to the establishment of high productivity assembly plants exporting to the United States market – especially those producing automobile engines – in the first half of the 1980s. These plants, along with other auto-parts assemblers producing under the *maquiladora* programme, benefited from tariff exemptions granted by the United States under its Harmonized Tariff System 9802. Between 1979 and 1986, foreign firms established about 40 affiliates in northern Mexican border towns for assembling parts for re-export (Romijn, Van Assouw and Mortimore, 2000: 144). In the second half of the 1980s and early 1990s, both domestic sales and exports of passenger cars increased considerably. By 1994, exports accounted for well over half of all passenger cars produced. Moreover, there was a significant rise in the share of vehicles in total exports, from 10 per cent in 1985 to about 65 per cent by the early 1990s, when other foreign producers began to see Mexico as a potential platform from which to enter the United States market.

The early surge in FDI was accompanied by a steep rise in imports. The high level of imported parts from the United States meant that the sector experienced only small trade surpluses, and even deficits, until 1994. Nevertheless, the Mexican industry had undergone a fairly dramatic restructuring, both in terms of productivity levels and export orientation, by the time NAFTA came into effect. NAFTA further deepened this restructuring process, as it not only provided preferences that benefited United States TNCs in the automobile industry, but it also extended regional rules of origin to producers of non-American origin, including component producers. In addition, the devaluation of the peso in connection with the financial crisis in 1994–1995 gave a sharp boost to exports when domestic sales collapsed. The prolonged United States boom in the second half of the 1990s firmly consolidated the position of Mexican producers as part of the regional industrial bloc. By the end of the decade, over two thirds of production was exported to the United States and trade surpluses had become the norm for the sector. Cross-border trade flows rose twelvefold between 1986 and 1999, compared with an average ninefold increase in total trade between the United States and Mexico, and a fivefold increase in Mexico's total trade. The surge in exports from the United States to Mexico during the second half of the 1990s was a strong indication of the rationalization of production by United States automobile manufacturers within an integrated North American production system.

NAFTA thus appears to have consolidated a process of regional restructuring by leading United States producers who sought to defend their domestic market share. Both cost advantages and policy incentives led them to intensify production sharing with offshore assembly sites. A series of conjunctural macroeconomic factors also contributed to Mexico's export growth. However, because the overall pattern has been driven by the needs of United States TNCs, weak linkages with domestic producers, low value added and a heavy reliance on a single market have given rise to concerns with regard to Mexico's own industrial development. In particular, the Mexican components industry remains heavily concentrated in the labour-intensive processes of engine castings and wiring harnesses, although some upgrading is expected in the production of more complex parts such as transmissions (USITC, 1999a). Local content is particularly low among the *maquiladora* auto-parts assemblers, but even outside the border areas over two thirds of components are sourced outside Mexico (Romijn, Van Assouw and Mortimore, 2000).[33]

The surge in automobile exports after 1995 was helped by an undervalued currency and stagnant real wages that have kept real relative manufacturing labour costs low. Real wages in manufacturing in Mexico, which had been falling during the initial switch to a more export-oriented automotive sector in the second half of the 1980s, rose modestly prior to the currency crisis of 1994, but fell back to the level of the early 1980s for the remainder of the decade. Thus macroeconomic pressures, through exchange rate movements or wage trends, remain potential sources of vulnerability.

---

[33] A new generation of *maquiladora* parts producers has emerged recently with the casting-off by Ford and General Motors of their in-house parts producers.

References

Arndt SW and Kierzkowski H, eds. (2001). *Fragmentation: New Production Patterns in the World Economy.* Oxford, Oxford University Press.

Athukorala P and Menon J (1997). AFTA and the investment-trade nexus in ASEAN. *The World Economy,* 20: 159–174.

Baldone S, Sdogati F and Tajoli L (2001). Patterns and determinants of international fragmentation of production: Evidence from outward processing trade between the EU and Central Eastern European countries. *Weltwirtschaftliches Archiv,* 137: 80–104.

Belderbos R, Capannelli G and Fukao K (2001). Backward vertical linkages of foreign manufacturing firms: Evidence from Japanese multinationals. *World Development,* 29: 189–208.

BLS (1997). *Handbook of Methods.* Washington, DC, United States Bureau of Labor Statistics, Department of Labor.

Choudhri EU and Hakura DS (2000). International trade and productivity growth: Exploring the sectoral effects for developing countries. IMF Staff Papers, 47: 30–53. Washington, DC, International Monetary Fund.

ECE (1995). *Economic Bulletin for Europe,* 47. United Nations publication, sales no. E.95.II.E.24, New York and Geneva, Economic Commission for Europe.

ECLAC (1999). *Foreign Investment in Latin America and the Caribbean. 1999 Report.* United Nations publication, sales no. E.00.II.G.4, Santiago, Chile, Economic Commission for Latin America and the Caribbean.

Ernst D (1997). From partial to systemic globalization: International production networks in the electronics industry. BRIE Working Paper, 98. Berkeley Roundtable on the International Economy, Berkeley, CA, April (http://brie.berkeley.edu/~briewww/pubs/wp/wp98.html).

Ernst D (1998). Catching-up, crisis and industrial upgrading. Evolutionary aspects of technological learning in Korea's electronics industry. Working Paper, 98–16. Aalborg, Denmark, Aalborg University, Danish Research Unit for Industrial Dynamics (DRUID) (http://www.business.auc.dk/druid/wp/pdf_files/98-16.pdf).

Ernst D (2000). Inter-organizational knowledge outsourcing: What permits small Taiwanese firms to compete in the computer industry? *Asia Pacific Journal of Management,* 17(2).

Ernst D and Guerrieri P (1998). International production networks and changing trade patterns in East Asia: The case of the electronics industry. *Oxford Development Studies,* 26.

Ernst D and Ravenhill J (1999). Globalization, convergence and the transformation of international production networks in electronics in East Asia. *Business and Politics,* 1: 35–62.

Finger JM and Schuknecht L (1999). Market access advances and retreats: The Uruguay Round and beyond. Working Paper, 2232. Washington, DC, World Bank.

Gereffi G (1999). International trade and industrial upgrading in the apparel commodity chain. *Journal of International Economics*, 48: 37–70.

Gordon RJ (2000). Does the 'New Economy' measure up to the great inventions of the past? *Journal of Economic Perspectives*, 14: 49–79.

Graziani G (2001). International subcontracting in the textile and clothing industry. In: Arndt SW and Kierzkowski H, eds. *Fragmentation: New Production Patterns in the World Economy*. Oxford, Oxford University Press.

Hanson GH, Mataloni RJ and Slaughter MJ (2002). Expansion strategies of U.S. multinational firms. In: Collins SM and Rodrik D, eds. *Brookings Trade Forum 2001*. Washington, DC, Brookings Institution.

Hummels D, Ishii J and Yi KM (2001). The nature and growth of vertical specialization in world trade. *Journal of International Economics*, 54: 75–96.

Hummels D, Rapoport D and Yi K-M (1998). Vertical specialization and the changing nature of world trade. *Economic Policy Review*. New York, Federal Reserve Bank, June: 79–99.

Jaffee S and Gordon P (1993). Exporting high-value food commodities: Success stories from developing countries. Discussion Paper, 198. Washington, DC, World Bank.

Laird S and Yeats A (1990). Trends in nontariff barriers of developed countries, 1966–1986. *Weltwirtschaftliches Archiv*, 126: 299–235.

Lall S (1995). Industrial strategy and policies on foreign direct investment in East Asia. *Transnational Corporations*, 4(3), December.

Lall S (1998). Exports of manufactures by developing countries: Emerging patterns of trade and location. *Oxford Review of Economic Policy*, 14(2): 54–73.

Low P and Yeats A (1995). Nontariff measures and developing countries: Has the Uruguay Round leveled the playing field? *The World Economy*, 18: 51–70.

Mayer J, Butkevicius A and Kadri A (2002). Dynamic products in world exports. UNCTAD Discussion Paper No. 159. May. Geneva.

Miozzo M (2000). Transnational corporations, industrial policy and the 'war of incentives': The case of the Argentine automobile industry. *Development and Change*, 31: 651–680.

Miranda J, Torres RA and Ruiz M (1998). The international use of antidumping: 1987–1997. *Journal of World Trade*, 32(5): 5–71.

Mortimore M, Lall S, Romijn H, with Laraki K, Martinez E, Vicens LJ and Zamora R (2000). The garment industry. In: UNCTAD, *The Competitiveness Challenge: Transnational Corporations and Industrial Restructuring in Developing Countries.* United Nations publication, sales no. E.00.II.D.35, New York and Geneva.

Mortimore M, Romijn H and Lall S, with Ariff M, Carillo J and Yew SY (2000). The colour TV receiver industry. In: UNCTAD, *The Competitiveness Challenge: Transnational Corporations and Industrial Restructuring in Developing Countries.* United Nations publication, sales no. E.00.II.D.35, New York and Geneva.

Ng F and Yeats A (1999). Production sharing in East Asia: Who does what for whom and why? Policy Research Working Paper, 2197, Washington, DC, World Bank, October. Also in: Cheng LK and Kierzkowski H, eds. (2001). *Global Production and Trade in East Asia.* Boston, Kluwer Academic Publishers.

Nicita A and Olarreaga M (2001). Trade and Production, 1976–99. Working Paper, 2701. Washington, DC, World Bank, 6 November.

Oliner SO and Sichel DE (2000). The resurgence of growth in the late 1990s: Is information technology the story? *Journal of Economic Perspectives*, 14: 3–22.

Oxford Analytica Brief (2002). East Asia: Manufacturing questions (http://www.oxweb.com/default.asp), 14 January.

Page S (1994). *How Developing Countries Trade. The Institutional Constraints.* London and New York, Routledge.

Preusse HG (2001). MERCOSUR – Another failed move towards regional integration. *The World Economy*, 24: 911–931.

Rodrik D (1999). Response to Srinivasan and Bhagwati: Outward-orientation and development: Are revisionists right? Mimeo. Cambridge, MA, Harvard University.

Romijn H, Van Assouw R and Mortimore M, with Carrillo J, Lall S and Poapongsakorn N (2000). TNCs, industrial upgrading and competitiveness in the automotive industry in NAFTA, MERCOSUR and ASEAN. In: UNCTAD, *The Competitiveness Challenge: Transnational Corporations and Industrial Restructuring in Developing Countries.* United Nations publication, sales no. E.00.II.D.35, New York and Geneva.

Srinivasan TN and Bhagwati J (1999). Outward-orientation and development: Are revisionists right? Economic Growth Center Discussion Paper, 806. New Haven, CT, Yale University, September.

Streeten P (1993). The multinational enterprise and the theory of development policy. In: Lall S, ed. *Transnational Corporations and Economic Development.* United Nations Library on Transnational Corporations, vol. 3. London and New York, Routledge.

UNCTAD (2000). *Handbook of Statistics*. United Nations publication, sales no. E.00.II.D.30, New York and Geneva.

UNCTAD (2001). *World Investment Report, 2001*. United Nations publication, sales no. E.01.II.D.12. New York and Geneva.

UNCTAD/ECLAC (2002). Summary and conclusions. UNCTAD/ECLAC Joint Regional Seminar on FDI Policies in Latin America, 7–9 January, Santiago, Chile (www.ECLAC.org/).

UN/DESA (various issues). *Monthly Bulletin of Statistics*. New York, United Nations Department of Economic and Social Affairs (http://esa.un.org/unsd/mbs/mbssearch.asp).

UNIDO (various issues). *Handbook of Industrial Statistics*. Vienna, United Nations Industrial Development Organization.

UNIDO (various issues). *International Yearbook of Industrial Statistics*. Vienna, United Nations Industrial Development Organization.

United States Census Bureau (2001). *Statistics for Industry Groups and Industries,1999. Annual Survey of Manufacturers*. Washington, DC, United States Department of Commerce, May (http://www.census.gov/prod/2001pubs/m99-as1.pdf).

USITC (1999a). *Production Sharing: The Use of U.S. Components and Materials in Foreign Assembly Operations, 1995–1998*. USITC Publication, 3265. Washington, DC, United States International Trade Commission, December.

USITC (1999b). *Industry and Trade Summary: Apparel*. USITC Publication, 3169, Washington, DC, United States International Trade Commission, March.

World Bank (1994). *Global Economic Prospects and the Developing Countries*. Washington, DC.

World Bank (2000). *World Development Indicators 2000*. Washington, DC (http://www.worldbank.org/data/wdi/home.html).

WTO (1998). *Trade Policy Review: European Union 1997*. Geneva, World Trade Organization.

WTO (2001). *Market Access: Unfinished Business. Post-Uruguay Round Inventory and Issues*. Special Studies, 6. Geneva, World Trade Organization.

Yeats A (2001). Just how big is global production sharing? In: Arndt SW and Kierzkowski H, eds. *Fragmentation: New Production Patterns in the World Economy*. Oxford, Oxford University Press.

Chapter 2

COMPETITION AND THE FALLACY OF COMPOSITION

A. The issues at stake

The standard advice to developing countries experiencing difficulties in promoting primary sector exports is to move to labour-intensive manufacturing. Such a strategy is advocated on a number of grounds. First, since labour is in more plentiful supply in most developing countries than natural resources, there is more scope for expanding production based on labour than on natural resources. This proposition, which draws on the traditional theory of comparative advantage, is probably valid for most developing countries outside Africa; in that region comparative advantage lies more in natural resources (*TDR 1998*, Part Two, chap. IV). Second, it is easier to upgrade to technology- and capital-intensive activities and to supply-dynamic products from low-skill, labour-intensive manufacturing than from primary production. Again, this is generally correct. However, the evidence surveyed in chapter 1 shows that many of the developing countries involved in the labour-intensive segments of international production networks have not been able to make much progress in graduating to more sophisticated manufactures. The third reason posited in favour of labour-intensive manufacturing activities is that demand for these products is more stable than the demand for primary products. Again, the evidence reviewed in the previous chapter, on the volatility of export values of products around their longer-term trends and on the behaviour of export and import prices of the United States, confirms the validity of this proposition. However, it is also true that in recent years a number of manufactures, notably in computers and electronics, have shown extreme volatility, causing serious disruptions in the export earnings and external payments of a number of developing economies in East Asia.

Perhaps one of the most important reasons for moving into labour-intensive manufactures is that these products are more market-dynamic than primary commodities: they offer better prospects for expansion of volume of exports without incurring a serious risk of sharply falling prices and/or earnings because of low price elasticities of demand. Again, the evidence examined in the previous chapter generally confirms this proposition, but it is also true that world trade in a number of primary commodities has been growing faster than that in many manufactures, mainly of the labour-intensive kind. The issue remains, however, of the threshold beyond which an expansion of exports will lead to a sharp drop in prices. This is the well-known problem of fallacy of composition, or the adding-up problem: that is, on its own a small developing country can substantially expand its exports without flooding the market and seriously reducing the prices of the products concerned, but this may not be true for developing countries as a whole, or even for large individual countries such as China and India. A rapid increase in exports of labour-intensive products involves a potential risk that the terms of trade will decline to such an extent that the benefits of any increased volume of exports may be more than offset by losses due to lower export prices, giving rise to "immiserizing growth" (Bhagwati, 1958).

A further complication is that the exporting countries may not be better off, even when rising export volumes offset falling net barter terms of trade (NBTT) and their export earnings or the purchasing power of their exports (i.e. income terms of trade) grow. Indeed, it is doubtful whether the concept of income terms of trade can meaningfully describe the benefits of such trade unless it is assumed that an additional volume of exports can be produced without additional resource costs. This might be the case when there is no alternative use for the labour employed in manufacturing for export and when there is no additional resource cost necessitating payment in foreign exchange. However, as seen in the previous chapter, the direct and indirect import contents of manufactured exports of developing countries are generally high; moreover, they have been rising in recent years, particularly in countries that have been pursuing rapid trade liberalization and participating in the labour-intensive segments of international production networks. Under these conditions, falling export prices and NBTT can entail resource losses, even though increasing volumes more than compensate for the fall in prices.

The evidence above shows that, with some notable exceptions, exports of developing countries have been concentrated in resource-based and labour-intensive products. This is true not only for many traditional manufactures, but also for what appear to be skill- and technology-intensive exports. Furthermore, it has also been noted that a large number of countries have not yet made significant inroads into markets for labour-intensive manufactures or participated to any great extent in the labour-intensive segments of international production networks. Even countries that have been highly active and successful on both fronts, such as China, still have large amounts of unemployed or underemployed low-skilled labour, which can potentially be used for increasing activity in traditional manufacturing sectors or international production networks. Thus fallacy of composition in labour-intensive manufactures may become a problem if there is a simultaneous export drive by developing countries in these manufactures, which would result in falling export prices and/or earnings. It can also become a problem, reflected in falling wages, when there is increased competition among these countries as locations for foreign direct investment (FDI) in simple processes of otherwise high-tech activities organized in international production networks. Government policies can exacerbate the problem by offering transnational corporations (TNCs) tax concessions and other incentives. The question of the probability of markets for labour-intensive manufactured exports from developing countries becoming oversupplied, and especially the policy responses this would call for, are thus important elements in the design of export-oriented development strategies. This chapter addresses these issues.

The next section reviews the empirical evidence concerning the behaviour of manufacturing terms of trade of developing countries vis-à-vis industrial countries over the past two decades. The evidence does not show an unambiguous, strongly downward trend threatening to reach the point of immiserizing growth. However, there are signs that prices of manufactured exports of developing countries have been weakening vis-à-vis those of industrial countries, especially for the less skill-intensive manufactured exports. Section C provides a comparative analysis of the degree of competition and concentration in markets for products exported by industrialized and developing countries and an examination of the profile of the global labour force participating in international trade, with a view to determining the extent of potential competition in labour-intensive products. It shows that competition is greater in markets for manufactures exported by developing countries, and that this could increase significantly; such a trend could lead to problems associated with fallacy of composition if the recent growth in the share of low-skilled workers involved in international trade continues unabated.

Whether these trends actually do lead to fallacy of composition depends, however, on a number of other factors, as was indicated by the results of simulations undertaken in the context of a North-South trade model in *TDR 1996* (Part Two, chap. III). Such factors include, *inter alia*, market access conditions for these products, the pace at which the more advanced developing countries diversify their own production structures away from low-skilled exports, and how quickly developed country producers move out of low-skill products (see also Havrylyshyn, 1990, and Martin, 1993). The analysis in section D shows that trade barriers in industrial countries discriminate against developing country manufactures, and that their removal could greatly increase the demand for these products. However, the problems faced in industrialized countries' labour markets, including high levels of unemployment among low-skilled workers and/or widening wage differentials and income inequality, tend to lead to pressures for increased protectionism against labour-intensive exports of developing countries, which, if heeded, would increase the risk of fallacy of composition.[1]

Faster growth in industrialized countries can help not only by expanding markets for the exports of developing countries, but also by creating job opportunities for their own labour. This would, of course, call for the adoption by the major industrialized countries of expansionary macroeconomic policies aimed at attaining the kind of rapid and sustained growth that could help alleviate their labour market problems. Rapid growth in these countries would need to be accompanied by structural policies designed to train labour to enable it to shift to more skilled activities.

A gradual, progressive move by developing countries at different levels of development across the spectrum of manufacturing industries – in the way described in the East Asian context as "the flying geese" process – can also help avert the problems associated with fallacy of composition and protectionist reactions by expanding South-South trade in manufactures and allowing newcomers some space in the markets of industrial countries (*TDR 1996*, Part Two, chap. I). In fact, the exit of some of the successful NIEs in Asia from low-skill, labour-intensive manufactures has already helped to create room for the new generation of NIEs in the region, as well as China. However, it is much more difficult to coordinate such a progressive division of labour at the global level than at the regional level; it requires a rapid upgrading by a significant number

---

[1] For instance, in an earlier study, Cline (1982) showed that if all developing countries had experienced the same export/GDP ratios as the first-tier NIEs, their exports would have captured 61 per cent of the developed country market in 1976, compared to the actual 17 per cent. It was argued that the acceptable threshold level for import penetration ratio was in the order of 15 per cent, and consequently any attempt to go well beyond that would have been thwarted by protectionism.

of middle-level countries into more sophisticated manufactures. Thus appropriate action is needed not only at the national level, but also in the multilateral forums to allow greater policy space for developing countries to support technological upgrading and progress.

Again, an appropriate balance in developing countries between reliance on domestic markets and exports can help. The difficulty here is that, as discussed at greater length in *TDR 1999*, many developing countries which have long neglected exports have felt the need for a rapid shift towards outward orientation to correct for past policy mistakes; this need is given greater urgency due to rapid import liberalization, widened current account imbalances, unstable private capital flows and diminished official aid. Furthermore, there is also the concern that greater emphasis on domestic markets could be seen as opening the door to protectionism and as implying opposition to global integration.

Rhetoric aside, history teaches that the economic development of the United States, Japan and almost all of the Western European countries was based on their home markets. Apart from some small economies (such as Ireland), none of the advanced countries has a manufacturing sector that is as highly export-oriented as it is in fairly large developing countries both in Asia and Latin America. Moreover, as seen in the previous chapter, in a number of advanced economies (e.g. France, Germany, Japan and the United States) the ratio of manufactured exports to manufacturing value added has, for some years, been fairly stable at a relatively low level. This suggests that the outward orientation of certain developing countries may decline as they grow richer and their home markets expand, and it implies that their domestic sales will grow even faster than their exports of manufactures. This seems inevitable in the case of a large country like China, but it may also be true for countries like Mexico and Malaysia. If so, the large share of exports in total output of many developing economies represents a stage of development that economies go through before their home markets mature. Managing that stage to avoid a fallacy of composition is a challenge to development policy and development cooperation.

B.   The terms of trade of developing country exports: a review of the evidence

Following the work of Prebisch and Singer, it has frequently been argued that the terms of trade between non-fuel primary commodities and manufactures are on a downward trend. Several studies on the fallacy of composition thesis for exports of primary commodities have found support for this argument with respect to a number of agricultural commodities, in particular bananas, cocoa, coffee, cotton, tea and tobacco, but also some other commodities such as copper and petroleum (Bleaney, 1993; Akiyama and Larson, 1994; World Bank, 1996: 55; and *TDR 1993*: 98–102). Export earnings from these commodities are of vital importance to a wide range of developing countries, and oversupply has involved substantial revenue losses for them in recent decades. Accordingly, they have been advised to diversify away from primary products into manufactures, for which income and price elasticities of demand are considered to be comparatively high.

The downward trend in the terms of trade for commodities certainly remains a crucial concern for a large number of developing countries, as it affects their capacity to import essential goods for their development. However, as noted above, many developing countries in Asia and Latin America have experienced rapid growth in manufactured exports; at the aggregate level, the value of these exports to developed countries has exceeded that of their primary commodity exports since the early 1990s. As a consequence, the debate on terms of trade has increasingly turned towards the relative movements in the prices (or unit values) of manufactures exported by developing countries vis-à-vis those exported by developed countries.

This shift in the debate from terms of trade between primary commodities and manufactures to those between manufactures and other manufactures has been accompanied by a shift in the analysis of the underlying factors. The Prebisch-Singer hypothesis focuses on the characteristics of the products traded (primary products versus manufactures); it emphasizes that income elasticity of demand for primary commodities is lower than for manufactures, and that there is an upward supply bias for commodities due to the existence of a large pool of unemployed or underemployed labour in developing countries. By contrast, the more recent debate relates primarily to the characteristics of the trading parties (developed versus developing countries), emphasizing their differences in terms of technological capacity, labour market institutions and the absence or presence of surplus labour. From this perspective, the types of manufactures exported by developing countries, compared to those exported by developed countries, are said to share some of the disadvantages which were originally associated in the Prebisch-Singer hypothesis concerning primary products in comparison with manufactures. This change in focus has important policy implications because, to the extent that developing countries face a downward trend in their terms of trade in manufactures, an outward-oriented industrialization strategy based on a shift from primary to manufactured exports may fail to solve their terms-of-trade problem.

An early study on terms of trade in manufactures found that, over the period 1970–1987, the price of manufactured exports from developing countries had fallen by an average of 1 per cent a year relative to the price of manufactured exports from developed countries (Sarkar and Singer, 1991). This finding has been challenged on the grounds that, through rapid expansion of their manufactured exports, developing countries have achieved significant gains in their purchasing power of exports; moreover, the apparent deterioration in their terms of trade in manufactures virtually disappears when non-ferrous metals are excluded from the definition of manufactures (Athukorala, 1993). According to this view, non-ferrous metals should be treated as primary commodities because their manufacturing value-added component is small and because variations in their price mainly reflect variations in the price of metalliferous ores. However, further studies have shown that relative prices of non-ferrous metals have behaved in a more or less similar way as other manufactured exports of developing countries for much of the period, following an unusually large fall in the early 1970s, when these metals accounted for a large share of developing country exports. There is evidence of a decline in developing countries' terms of trade in manufactures since 1975, regardless of whether non-ferrous metals are classified as primary commodities or manufactures (Rowthorn, 1997). This result is supported by a study comparing a price index of manufactured exports from developing countries with a price index for the combined exports of services and complex manufactures from developed countries (where non-ferrous metals are not included among manufactures). The study shows a large, though unsteady and irregular, deterioration in the manufacturing terms of trade of developing countries since 1960, occurring mainly in the 1960s, but falling again between 1985 and 1990 (Minford, Riley and Nowell, 1997).

Further support for the hypothesis of a deterioration of developing countries' terms of trade in manufactures is provided by an analysis for the period 1979–1994 using the unit values of manufactured imports and exports between the EU and developing countries (Maizels, Palaskas, and Crowe, 1998).[2] This study also provides a first empirical test of the proposition that scientific and technological capacities have a major impact on the development of terms of trade (Singer, 1975). It does so by analyzing the terms of trade in manufactures of the EU with different groups of countries at different stages of scientific and technological development, including selected developing country groups, Japan and the United States. The examination of the NBTT, measured in terms of the ratio between unit value indices of imports and exports of manufactures, suggests that both the United States and Japan – the world leaders in a wide range of technology-intensive manufactures – experienced a slightly favourable trend in their manufactures' terms of trade with the EU. A moderately negative trend was observed for East and South-East Asia (with their NBTT deteriorating at less than 1 per cent a year), but there was a strong negative trend for the least developed countries (LDCs) and the African, Caribbean and Pacific (ACP) group of countries, with a decline of 5 per cent a year. Latin American and Mediterranean countries were in-between, in accordance with the level of their scientific and technological development and skill-content of their manufactured exports.[3] The analysis of the previous chapter suggests that these different trends do not reflect differential productivity growth rates, since the supply dynamism of manufactures exported by lesser developed countries is low compared to that of the more skill- and technology-intensive products.

Similar conclusions were reached by a study on the evolution of the Republic of Korea's terms of trade in manufactures with less and more advanced countries for the period 1976–1995 (Berge and Crowe, 1997). The results indicate no significant trend in the NBTT of the Republic of Korea regarding its trade in manufactures with advanced industrial countries, but a significant increase vis-à-vis other developing countries,

---

[2] These findings also show that the sharp expansion in the volume of the EU's imports of manufactures from developing countries more than offsets the deterioration in the NBTT, which has resulted in an improvement in the purchasing power of manufactured exports of developing countries or their income terms of trade.

[3] The composition of the different groups is as follows: East and South-East Asia comprises the four NIEs (Hong Kong (China), the Republic of Korea, Singapore and Taiwan Province of China), the ASEAN-4 (Indonesia, Malaysia, the Philippines and Thailand), as well as Brunei and Macao (China). The group of LDCs comprises 37 low-income countries, of which 27 are in sub-Saharan Africa. The composition of the ACP group overlaps with the group of LDCs to a considerable extent. The group of Mediterranean countries comprises Algeria, Cyprus, Egypt, Israel, Jordan, Lebanon, Malta, Morocco, Tunisia, Turkey and the former Yugoslavia.

and an even greater increase in the income terms of trade. This suggests that the exports of the Republic of Korea have increasingly shifted to higher value-added, technologically sophisticated, dynamic manufactures, compared to the basic manufactures exported by its less developed trading partners, and that technological upgrading can have a major influence on the movement of the terms of trade not only between developed and developing countries, but also among developing countries.

An analysis of the medium-term trends over the period 1981–1996 in the terms of trade in manufactures of developing and developed countries with respect to the United States constitutes a further piece of evidence (Maizels, 2000). This analysis was based on one of the most reliable data sets on trade prices, namely the new price series compiled and published by the United States Bureau of Labor Statistics (BLS).[4] The study arrives at two main results. First, by examining the behaviour of the United States NBTT with developing and other developed countries, it concludes that the trend in the terms of trade of developing countries vis-à-vis developed countries as a whole has significantly worsened since the early 1980s.[5] Second, changes in the trade balance of manufactures of both developed and developing countries with the United States have been driven by the rapid growth in their volume. The volume

---

[4] These new time series are the result of considerable effort to ensure that the indices reflect only price changes and are not affected by quality changes. However, the BLS has compiled these series only since 1990, and for a limited number of economies (Canada, the EU, Japan and the first-tier NIEs); import price series for manufactured goods from Latin America have been compiled since December 1997. To provide a realistic medium-term trend, it is necessary to extend the series backwards to 1981 in order to obtain a complete data set for the period 1981–1996. For details on the method used to calculate and adjust the price-index series, see Maizels (2000: 6–11 and 27–36).

[5] The United States NBTT shows divergent trends vis-à-vis developing and developed countries; it rose significantly against developing countries in the first half of the 1980s but showed no distinct trend thereafter, whereas against the developed countries it was trendless in the first half of the 1980s, but rose significantly thereafter. Over the whole period, prices of the United States manufactured imports from developed countries (mainly automobiles and machinery) rose significantly faster than prices of imports from developing countries (mainly clothing), while prices of its manufactured exports to developed countries rose more slowly than prices of exports to developing countries. Maizels (2000: 17–21) shows that the price dispersion on any of the main manufactured products traded by the United States is much higher for its imports than for its exports; as he notes, this could indicate that price changes in exports are driven by domestic developments, such as growth rates in productivity and inflation rates, while price changes in imports are driven by international factors, such as changes in exchange rates, productivity and production costs across various national sources of supply.

increase in developing country exports has more than offset the declines in their NBTT.

An UNCTAD study shows that China's net barter terms of trade in manufactures deteriorated by more than 10 per cent over the period 1993–2000 (Zheng and Yumin, 2002) and that this deterioration was greater vis-à-vis developed countries than developing countries. Overall, it appears to have been less pronounced for traditional, labour-intensive manufactures than for products with medium and high technology intensity, such as computers and office equipment, as well as telecommunications equipment and semiconductors. These are the sectors in which China's participation in global production networks has grown the most rapidly over the past few years. But since China participates primarily in the labour-intensive segments of these networks, it is not surprising that the terms of trade in these products moved differently for China than for developed countries. The decline in its terms of trade for labour-intensive and resource-based manufactures was greatest with the United States and Japan, the world's most technologically advanced countries. It is also noteworthy that China's terms of trade in manufactures with high technology intensity deteriorated considerably vis-à-vis the countries of the Association of South-East Asian Nations (ASEAN), while they improved slightly with the United States. This finding reflects a triangular pattern of production sharing in computers and office equipment, as well as in telecommunications equipment and semiconductors; since China imports inputs from the ASEAN countries and re-exports them, with little domestic value added, to the United States, higher prices of inputs imported from ASEAN translate into higher prices in the processed products exported to the United States.

The empirical evidence thus strongly suggests that global competition for labour-intensive manufacturing activities has risen over the past few years. This coincides with the shift in the mid-1980s of several highly populated, low-income economies towards more export-oriented strategies. The countries with the lowest proportion of technology-intensive manufactures and the greatest proportion of low-skill, labour-intensive products in their manufactured exports have faced declining terms of trade in manufactures. A few others appear to have succeeded in improving their terms of trade vis-à-vis lesser developed countries by upgrading their exports into higher skill- and technology-intensive products. Intensification of clustering at the low end of manufactured exports and increased competition for markets for them might strengthen these divergent trends.

C. Competition in world markets for labour-intensive manufactures

It is generally held that prices of manufactures are much less flexible than prices of primary commodities in world trade, in large part because markets for manufactures are much less competitive, and because of the greater ease with which supply of manufactures can respond to fluctuations in demand. Most markets for manufactures have high barriers to entry; many are oligopolistic, controlled by a small number of producers who often compete on the basis of quality, design, marketing, branding and product differentiation rather than prices. In such markets prices move more in line with supply conditions and costs than with fluctuations in the level of demand. Firms tend to respond to variations in demand by adjusting their inventories and production rather than their prices; indeed, consumers may even face rationing in the form of queues or delays between orders and delivery. Firms often target a certain mark-up over costs, especially labour costs. In most major industrial countries, wages in firms are not flexible, which means that price declines cannot be easily passed on to labour in order to maintain profit margins; this is true even in countries considered as having flexible labour markets. This inflexibility is not only due to a number of labour market regulations, including minimum wage legislation, collective bargaining and restrictions on hiring and firing; it is often also embedded in established industrial practices and traditions designed to provide secure and predictable incomes for workers.

The absence of such conditions in the labour markets of most developing countries, at least for low-skilled labour, together with large amounts of surplus labour, often implies that wages there are much more flexible than in industrial countries. This increases the ability of firms to lower wages when there are price declines so that profit margins are not sacrificed; it thus allows them to compete on the basis of prices in markets for labour-intensive manufactures. In a sense, therefore, competition among firms located in developing countries in world markets for labour-intensive manufactures becomes competition among labour located in different countries. The combination of increased mobility of capital and mass unemployment and underemployment in the developing world weakens the bargaining position of labour even in countries that enjoy full employment. Furthermore, the East Asian experience noted in the previous chapter shows that mobility of low-skilled labour is greater among developing countries than between

Table 2.1

**MANUFACTURES WITH THE LOWEST MARKET
CONCENTRATION IN WORLD TRADE, 1997–1998**

Rank	SITC code	Product group	Index of concentration 1997–1998	Rank by rate of decrease in concentration 1990–1998
1	635	Wood manufactures	441	24
2	651	Textile yarn	458	86
3	941	Live animals	474	125
4	673	Iron and steel bars, and rods	487	118
5	693	Wire products and fencing grills	504	110
6	522	Inorganic chemicals	507	116
7	677	Iron or steel wires	518	127
8	691	Metal structures and parts	537	100
9	652	Cotton fabrics	555	113
10	771	Electric power machinery	560	3
11	846	Knitted undergarments	561	9
12	672	Iron or steel ingots and forms	569	103
13	843	Women's textile garments	571	85
14	692	Metal containers	578	88
15	671	Pig and sponge iron	582	94
16	842	Men's textile garments	600	35
17	845	Knitted outergarments	613	92
18	844	Textile undergarments	623	30
19	658	Made-up textile articles	631	52
20	679	Iron and steel castings	635	23
Memo item:				
34	764	Telecommunications equipment and parts	672	6
64	752	Computers	793	5
75	759	Parts of computers and office machines	855	10
87	776	Transistors and semiconductors	942	1
		All manufactured products (unweighted average)	957	

Source: UNCTAD secretariat calculations, based on UN/DESA, *Commodity Trade Statistics* database.
Note: The degree of market concentration for a particular product is expressed as the Herfindahl-Hirschman index (HHI) calculated for each product by taking the sum of the squared values of the market shares of all countries exporting that product, i.e. HHI$_j$ = $\Sigma(S_{ij})^2$ where S$_i$ is the share of country *i* expressed as a percentage of total world exports of product *j*. This means that the HHI ranges between 43, indicating that all 234 countries in the sample have equal shares (i.e. 0.43 per cent) in a product's total exports, and 10 000, indicating that the product is exported by only one country. The index numbers given are averages for 1997 and 1998.

developing and industrial countries. All these factors combined not only introduce greater price flexibility in the markets for developing countries' labour-intensive manufactures vis-à-vis those exported by industrial countries, but also exert a downward pressure on their prices and terms of trade. Without rapid productivity growth, the burden of adjustment naturally falls on labour.[6] In other words, labour-intensive manufactures exported by developing countries behave more like primary commodities than like skill-/technology-intensive manufactures.

In order to assess the degree of competition in world markets for different manufactures, table 2.1 ranks products according to their degree of concentration in export markets in 1997–1998.[7] The table shows that, together with iron and steel (SITC 67) and textiles (SITC 65), the clothing industry (SITC 84) was the sector with the lowest degree of market concentration: 5 of the 7 product groups in this sector were among the 20 products with the most equal distribution of market shares among exporting countries. It also suggests that the concentration in markets for dynamic electronic and electrical goods was lower than the average for all manufactured products. In other words, on this measure, markets for clothing and electronics have been more competitive than those for most other manufactures. Moreover, the decline in the concentration ratios for the dynamic electronic and electrical goods suggests that markets for these products became more competitive during the period 1990–1998. Indeed, the decline in the degree of concentration in these markets was among the highest of all manufactured products. As noted above, the production of these otherwise technology-intensive products includes labour-intensive processes, in which developing countries have increasingly participated in recent years. By contrast, finished products from technology-intensive activities such as machinery (e.g. non-electric engines and motors, and steam engines) or transport equipment (e.g. aircraft, ships and boats, motor cycles and passenger motor cars) were among those with the highest concentration of export market shares. The vast majority of exporters of these products are from developed countries.

---

[6] This is not to say that labour employed in export sectors in developing countries is necessarily worse off than that employed in their non-trading sectors, but that increased competition among developing countries in markets for low-skill manufactures exerts a downward pressure on manufacturing wages and prices. For the evidence on the impact of trade liberalization and export drive on wages in developing countries, see UNCTAD (2001a).
[7] Note that here concentration is measured in terms of shares of countries rather than firms, as is usually the case.

Chart 2.1

MARKET CONCENTRATION IN MAJOR WORLD EXPORT ITEMS, 1980-1998

A. Clothing

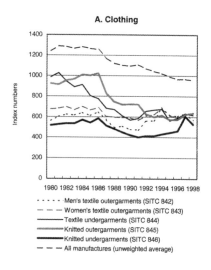

- - - - - Men's textile outergarments (SITC 842)
— — — Women's textile outergarments (SITC 843)
———— Textile undergarments (SITC 844)
════════ Knitted outergarments (SITC 845)
━━━━ Knitted undergarments (SITC 846)
— — — All manufactures (unweighted average)

B. Electronic products

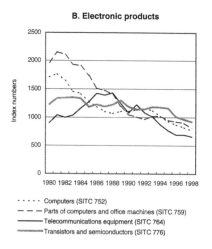

- - - - - Computers (SITC 752)
— — — Parts of computers and office machines (SITC 759)
———— Telecommunications equipment (SITC 764)
════════ Transistors and semiconductors (SITC 776)

Source: See table 2.1

Note: On the calculation of the degree of market concentration see note to table 2.1

Chart 2.2

SHARE OF SELECTED DEVELOPING COUNTRIES AND REGIONS IN
WORLD CLOTHING EXPORTS, 1980-1998

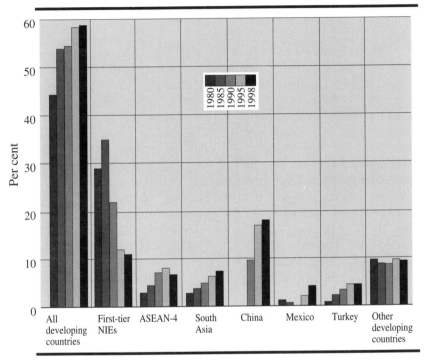

Source: See table 2.1.
Note: Clothing exports include SITC 842-846. South Asia includes Bangladesh, India,
Pakistan and Sri Lanka. Data for China for 1980 and 1985 are not available.

For the group of manufactured products taken together, the degree of
market concentration appears to have declined and competition to have
increased throughout the period 1981–1998, especially between the mid-
1980s and mid-1990s. The timing of such changes in the clothing sector
differed from that in the electronics sector (chart 2.1). In clothing, market
concentration changed little during the first half of the 1980s, but
declined continuously between 1987 and 1991, after which, for most of
the products in this group, it started to increase slightly. By contrast,
market concentration for the selected products from the electronics
industry declined throughout the period 1981–1998; this tendency was

particularly pronounced during the second half of the 1980s and of the 1990s. An exception is telecommunications equipment, where the degree of export market concentration rose significantly during the first half of the 1980s and then fell from 1989 onwards. A common characteristic of the clothing and electronics sectors is that the variation in the degree of concentration across markets for different products from these sectors drastically narrowed between 1981 and 1998.[8]

These developments are in line with the evolution of developing countries' participation in the production and export of labour-intensive manufactures. The share of developing countries in world exports grew considerably during the period 1980–1998 for both clothing and selected products from the electronics industry. However, the increase was concentrated in a small number of economies. The first-tier NIEs accounted for two thirds of all clothing exports from developing economies during the first half of the 1980s, but their share dropped thereafter to about one fifth by the mid-1990s, as they upgraded their exports and began to exit from the clothing markets (chart 2.2). Their market shares were taken up by other developing countries in Asia, notably those in South Asia, the ASEAN-4 (see note 3), China, Turkey and Mexico. This has been associated with lower concentration of market shares in clothing, indicating a tendency towards a greater degree of competition among developing countries, notably among the newcomers.

In the markets for the selected products from the electronics sector, first-tier NIEs were responsible for most of the spectacular increase in the share of developing countries in world exports between the 1980s and the mid-1990s: during this period, the share of these economies increased from two thirds to three fourths of all developing country exports of these products (chart 2.3). Other developing countries, such as the ASEAN-4, China and Mexico have succeeded in increasing their market shares in the past few years. The growing price competition in these products, especially in semiconductors, appears to have exposed the traditional developing country exporters to greater competition from lower cost suppliers in other developing countries.

Comparing the trends in the country-specific distribution of export market shares, it is interesting to note that the ASEAN-4 and China have

---

[8]   In the clothing sector the degree of concentration ranged between 527 and 1,027 in 1981, compared to a range between 528 and 637 in 1998. The respective index numbers for the selected products from the electronics industry ranged between 899 and 1,961 in 1980, and between 658 and 924 in 1998.

Chart 2.3

SHARE OF SELECTED DEVELOPING COUNTRIES AND REGIONS IN EXPORTS OF ELECTRONIC PRODUCTS,[a] 1980-1998

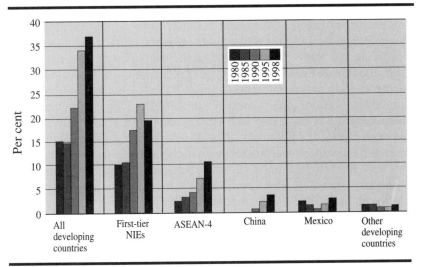

Source: See table 2.1.

Note: Data for China for 1980 and 1985 are not available.

[a] Computers (SITC 752), parts of computers and office machines (SITC 759), telecommunications equipment and parts (SITC 764), transistors and semiconductors (SITC 776).

gained market shares in the electronics sector much more rapidly than in clothing. Even though China started from a low base, and its absolute share in world exports of the selected products from the electronics industry is still low, a continuation of recent trends would suggest that China's share in world exports could grow much more in electronics than in clothing.

D. Skill profile of world trade and shifts in competitiveness

An important factor that may affect fallacy of composition in labour-intensive manufactures is the sharp increase in the number of low-skilled workers participating in trade-related activities. Given that most of the countries that have become increasingly integrated into the world trading system over the past few years are highly populated, low-income countries with labour endowments strongly skewed towards low-skilled labour, it is not surprising to find that the proportion of such labour embodied in the products traded in world markets has increased compared to high-skilled labour.

To analyze the impact of changes in the rate of participation of the world labour force in international trade and of its skill composition on the pattern of competitiveness in manufacturing across countries and geographical regions, it is convenient to classify a country's labour force according to three categories of skill: labour with no education (unskilled), with basic education (low-skilled), and with substantial post-elementary education and training (high-skilled).[9] Workers without any formal education are generally unsuitable for employment in manufacturing because they lack literacy and numeracy. The distinction between literate and illiterate workers is straightforward, but that between high-skilled workers and workers with basic skills is somewhat arbitrary; it is most likely to be found somewhere between incomplete and complete secondary education. This classification is inevitably a simplification; in reality, there is likely to be a continuum of skills which allows some substitution among workers with different levels of education.[10] Nonetheless, the classification is useful for identifying the order of magnitudes involved and for visualizing the general pattern of change in the skill composition of the labour force participating in world trade.

Chart 2.4 shows that the absolute numbers of unskilled, low-skilled and high-skilled workers participating in world trade have steadily increased over the past 25 years, reflecting the rapid growth in world trade and increased integration. However, the share of unskilled workers in the total labour force participating in world trade has dropped significantly. This reflects the marginalization in the context of world trade of countries with poor human capital. By contrast, the share of low-skilled labour involved in world trade increased, particularly between 1980 and 1990, rising from 64 per cent to 68 per cent, due to the greater participation of several highly populated low-income countries in world

---

[9] This classification follows Wood (1994). It is clear that equating the skill level of workers with their degree of formal education is inadequate because it ignores on-the-job learning and training. Moreover, cross-country comparisons of educational attainments ignore differences in the quality of formal education. However, comprehensive data that would take account of these aspects are not available.

[10] The scope for substitution depends on the degree to which skills are sector-specific, i.e. the result of the experience accumulated "on the job". Where this is the case, moving from one sector to another implies that workers lose part of their skill and thus part of their earning capability.

Chart 2.4

**SKILL COMPOSITION OF ADULT POPULATION PARTICIPATING IN WORLD
EXPORT PRODUCTION, 1975-2000**

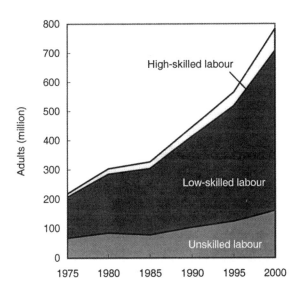

Source: UNCTAD secretariat calculations, based on Barro and Lee (2000), and UNCTAD,
    Handbook of Statistics (various issues).

  Note: Unskilled labour includes adults without schooling. Low-skilled labour includes adults with
    schooling up to complete secondary education. High-skilled labour includes adults with at
    least some tertiary schooling. The number of workers at a specific level of skills that are
    integrated into world exports is the sum of workers at a specific level of skills across all
    developing and developed countries for which comprehensive data are available (97
    countries) weighted by each country's ratio of exports to GDP.

trade. On the other hand, the increase in the share of high-skilled labour,
particularly between 1990 and 2000 (rising from about 7 per cent to 10
per cent), appears to reflect the growth in intra-industry trade among
developed countries, as well as greater production sharing between
developed countries and the first-tier NIEs.

An important consequence of the increase in the number of low-
skilled workers participating in world trade is that it has altered the
competitiveness of middle-income countries in manufacturing. In these
countries the ratio of high-skilled to low-skilled labour tends to be above

the average ratio for developing countries taken together, although it is below the average for developed countries. This gives the middle-income countries a competitive edge in low-skill manufactures, but they tend to lose this advantage once the highly populated developing countries with plenty of low-skilled workers become more active participants in world trade. Thus it is imperative that middle-income countries upgrade rapidly from low-skill to more market-dynamic, technology-intensive products with a view to successfully competing with industrialized countries and the first-tier NIEs. If not, they risk being squeezed between the bottom and top ends of the markets for manufactured exports.

Chart 2.5 indicates that countries in Latin America, and probably the second-tier NIEs, have indeed experienced such a squeeze. It shows movements in the skill mix of adult populations of various regions relative to the average skill mix of the total labour force involved in world trade. In the chart, a region which has the same skill mix as the world average would be located at point *A*. Regions located in the south-west quadrant of the chart have higher proportions of unskilled labour than the world average, while those in the north-east quadrant have lower proportions. A horizontal movement in an easterly direction indicates an increase in the region's proportion of low-skilled labour and a decrease in the share of unskilled labour relative to the world average. Countries moving in that direction would be entering into markets for low-skill-intensive manufactures or raising their shares in these markets. Similarly, a vertical movement in a northerly direction indicates an increase in the region's proportion of high-skilled labour and a decrease in the share of unskilled labour relative to the world average. Again countries moving in that direction would be shifting towards increasing their shares in markets for high-skill manufactures from markets for low-skill manufactures.

China and, in particular, the low-income countries of South Asia moved strongly eastwards, especially in the second half of the 1980s. This move reflects the increasing integration of these two groups into world trade as well as the fact that they have a high proportion of low-skilled workers, which gives them a competitive edge over Latin America and the second-tier East Asian NIEs in labour-intensive manufactures (*TDR 1998*, Part Two, chap. IV). This shift underlies, in part, the greater competition in world trade for low-skill manufactures, such as clothing, noted in the previous section. Chart 2.5 also suggests that China and the second-tier NIEs have been moving in a parallel fashion in building their competitiveness. Compared to the world average, for both groups of countries the growth in the number of high-skilled workers seems to have

Chart 2.5

**REGIONAL SKILL COMPOSITION OF ADULT POPULATION, RELATIVE TO
WORLD AVERAGE SKILL COMPOSITION IN EXPORT PRODUCTION, 1975-2000**

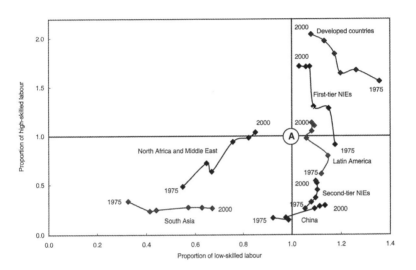

Source: See chart 2.4

Note: The chart shows the position of different regions, relative to the world average, which is
indicated by point A. For further explanations, see text.

outpaced that of workers with basic skills. This seems to indicate that, in
terms of composition of their manufactured exports, both groups of
countries have been gaining competitiveness in manufactures that require
medium to high skills, such as goods in the electronics sector or other
light manufactures. This is also consistent with the finding in the previous
section that competition in world markets for products in electronics has
increased considerably over the past few years. If this trend continues,
this sector will become even more competitive in the years to come.
Simulations suggest that in the next few years China's share in world
exports of electronics products and other light manufactures could be
substantial, and that this will occur independently of China's entry into

the World Trade Organization (WTO) (see, for example, Ianchovichina, Martin and Fukase, 2000: 36 and table 10).

E. Tariff barriers to exports of labour-intensive manufactures

1. Barriers in multilateral trading arrangements

As noted above, market access in labour-intensive manufactures is an important determinant of the risk presented by fallacy of composition in these products. Contrary to earlier expectations, developing countries have gained little from the Uruguay Round agreements in terms of access to the markets of industrial countries in these products. There have been some recent initiatives in this area, including preferential market access provided by the EU (the Everything-But-Arms Initiative) and the United States (the African Growth and Opportunity Act). These supplement existing non-reciprocal preferential agreements offered by developed countries, including Canada, Japan and the United States, as well as the EU. The new initiatives are certainly a step in the right direction, but the improved access they offer is restricted to the poorest countries.[11] Given that those countries generally are not large exporters of labour-intensive manufactures, the initiatives do little to improve market access for such exports.

The majority of developing countries with capacity to expand exports of labour-intensive manufactures continues to face significant barriers. Trade in textiles and clothing continues to be governed by quota regulations, and developing countries' manufactured exports encounter high tariffs and tariff escalation, as well as increased contingent forms of protection, notably anti-dumping action and new barriers, such as labour and environmental standards. Tariff peaks imposed by developed countries are often concentrated in products that are of export interest to developing countries;[12] they cover mainly labour-intensive manufactures: textiles, clothing, leather and rubber products, footwear and travel goods are subject to tariff peaks in Canada and the United States; and leather, rubber, footwear and travel goods in Japan. In the EU, tariff peaks concern mainly agricultural products, but leather, rubber, footwear and travel goods are the most affected categories within manufactures (WTO,

---

[11] For a discussion of these initiatives and their impact on market access for LDCs, see UNCTAD (2001b), and UNCTAD/Commonwealth Secretariat (2001).

[12] Tariff peaks are tariffs that exceed a selected reference level. They are often defined as tariff lines exceeding 15 per cent at the 6-digit level of the Harmonized System, following OECD (1999).

2001; UNCTAD/WTO, 2000). The significance of these tariff peaks for developing country exports is reflected in the fact that, taken together, clothing and footwear represent more than 60 per cent of tariff-peak-affected products exported from developing countries to the major industrial countries (Hoekman, Ng and Olarreaga, 2001: 7; also *TDR 1999*, Part Two, chap. VI). Moreover, most developed countries' tariffs increase with the level of processing, particularly for labour-intensive products such as textiles, clothing, leather and leather products (WTO, 2001: 36–39). Such products are often excluded from preferential tariff schemes – such as the Generalized System of Preferences (GSP) – or are subject to some kind of quantitative limitations, and imports from only selected countries are eligible for preferential rates. Thus many developing countries have little protection against tariff peaks and tariff escalation.

The previous chapter showed that trade in manufactures is expanding rapidly among developing countries themselves, and that access to each other's markets is becoming increasingly important. According to one view, developing countries themselves could significantly reduce the risk of fallacy of composition by lowering tariff barriers that affect exports of other developing countries. This argument is based on the observation that, despite considerable reform, applied tariffs on manufactures are, on average, higher in developing than in developed countries. However, such an argument could be relevant only with respect to high- and middle-income developing countries to the extent that they continue to produce labour-intensive manufactures behind tariff barriers, rather than upgrading their production and exports to skill-/technology-intensive products. Thus it is important to note the great variation in protection across developing countries; the level of protection through tariff and non-tariff measures is indeed lower in middle- and high-income than in low-income countries, and tariff liberalization has been especially impressive in a group of 15 to 20 middle- and high-income countries in Latin America and Asia.[13] This is important because, for the most part, middle- and high-income developing countries do not have a comparative advantage in producing labour-intensive manufactures, and also because the import demand for these products tends to be higher in countries at a comparatively higher level of income.

---

[13] Michalopoulos (1999) also notes the great variation in protection across developing countries. Balance-of-payments and fiscal considerations, rather than the desire to protect particular industries, appear to be the main reason why low-income countries maintain higher tariffs.

Tables 2.2 and 2.3 give simple and import-weighted most favoured nation (MFN) tariff rates as applied to selected categories of manufactured imports by developed and developing economies.[14] A comparison of the simple MFN average tariff rate on manufactured imports as a group with those applied in selected sectors (table 2.2) confirms that developed countries apply higher import tariffs to traditional labour-intensive manufactures (textiles, clothing, leather and travel goods, and footwear) than to other products, and that within the group of traditional labour-intensive manufactures import tariffs are highest for clothing and footwear. The comparison also shows that the low-income countries in Africa and Asia have, on average, higher tariffs than the middle- and high-income developing countries.

Comparing the tariff levels across different country groups, the table reveals that the first-tier NIEs apply, on average, lower tariffs than developed countries to all of the selected traditional labour-intensive manufacturing sectors. The tariffs applied by middle-income countries in East Asia and Latin America are much higher than those applied by the first-tier NIEs, which suggests that these countries are facing difficulties in industrial upgrading. However, the tariffs applied by leading developing country importers in East Asia (such as Indonesia, Malaysia, the Philippines) and Turkey are well within the range of developed country tariff rates in these sectors, and those applied, on average, in Latin America are not much higher than those in some of the developed countries.

Moreover, the simple average tariff rates applied in the traditional labour-intensive manufacturing sectors by a group of 22 high- and middle-income developing countries (which does not include the first-tier NIEs) are, in all cases, well within the 12 to 30 per cent range of the tariff rates applied to a large number of products in the textiles and clothing industries in Canada, the EU and the United States, and substantially lower than the tariff peaks in excess of 35 per cent applied to 10 per cent of the products in the footwear and leather products industries in Japan.[15] In addition, the simple tariff averages applied in the selected traditional

---

[14]   Tariff averages can be calculated using various weighting schemes. Simple tariff averages give equal weight to each tariff line. The relative importance of various tariff lines is better taken into account by tariff averages weighted according to import values, but they, nonetheless, have a downward bias, because imports of products that are subject to higher tariff rates will be lower than would otherwise be the case (i.e. an absolutely prohibitive tariff will have a zero weight). For these reasons, it is preferable to look at both simple and import-weighted averages.

[15]   The latter figures are from Michalopoulos (1999: 48).

Table 2.2

SIMPLE MFN AVERAGE TARIFFS OF SELECTED ECONOMIES, BY PRODUCT GROUP

(Per cent)

Importing economy/region	Manufactures (SITC 5–8 less 68)	Textiles (SITC 65)	Clothing (SITC 84)	Leather and travel goods (SITC 611, 612, 831)	Footwear (SITC 85)	Computers and office equipment (SITC 75)	Telecom, audio and video equipment (SITC 76)
Developed countries	**4.1**	**7.8**	**14.5**	**5.0**	**13.7**	**0.3**	**2.6**
Australia	5.4	9.9	20.7	4.7	11.1	0.3	5.4
Canada	4.9	10.7	18.4	4.2	16.3	0.2	1.5
European Union	4.4	7.9	11.4	3.3	12.4	0.8	4.1
Japan	2.9	6.5	11.0	10.2	19.2	0.0	0.0
New Zealand	3.1	2.4	13.7	2.7	9.5	0.3	3.0
United States	4.0	9.1	11.4	5.0	13.4	0.4	1.6
Developing economies							
First-tier NIEs	**3.6**	**4.5**	**6.4**	**2.8**	**4.3**	**2.3**	**4.3**
Hong Kong (China)	0.0	0.0	0.0	0.0	0.0	0.0	0.0
Republic of Korea	8.0	9.4	12.4	6.5	12.2	7.3	8.0
Singapore	0.0	0.0	0.0	0.0	0.0	0.0	0.0
Taiwan Province of China	6.4	8.3	13.1	4.6	5.0	1.6	8.1
ASEAN-4	**10.6**	**14.7**	**24.1**	**10.8**	**23.6**	**5.8**	**14.4**
Indonesia	9.0	12.6	18.1	8.8	17.8	3.8	13.9
Malaysia	9.9	16.7	19.6	9.5	26.8	2.0	13.1
Philippines	7.4	10.7	19.2	7.8	15.0	1.0	10.9
Thailand	16.1	18.7	39.7	17.3	34.8	16.4	19.5
South Asia	**21.4**	**24.2**	**29.4**	**22.1**	**33.6**	**14.0**	**22.3**
Bangladesh	22.1	30.2	..	17.1	..	9.4	22.5
India	34.1	39.0	40.0	32.3	40.0	28.9	37.0
Sri Lanka	8.0	3.4	11.0	17.0	23.2	3.6	7.4
Other Asia	**12.5**	**14.3**	**20.8**	**19.3**	**25.8**	**8.3**	**17.2**
China	9.6	9.7	16.1	13.0	20.4	4.0	13.7
Jordan	22.1	24.7	34.6	34.9	35.0	17.5	31.8
Turkey	5.9	8.6	11.8	10.0	22.1	3.5	6.3
Latin America	**11.9**	**15.8**	**20.8**	**14.1**	**20.8**	**8.3**	**13.6**
Argentina	16.1	20.1	22.9	17.4	33.0	12.3	18.6
Bolivia	9.6	10.0	10.0	10.0	10.0	10.0	10.0
Brazil	16.8	20.0	22.9	17.1	24.6	17.7	20.5
Chile	9.0	9.0	9.0	9.0	9.0	9.0	9.0
Colombia	12.1	18.0	19.9	13.1	20.0	5.1	13.3
Costa Rica	4.8	8.3	13.8	8.7	13.7	0.0	5.7
Dominican Republic	14.6	20.5	30.6	22.8	23.4	10.0	14.6
El Salvador	6.9	17.0	23.9	9.5	20.0	0.0	6.2
Jamaica	5.6	3.2	19.4	7.6	18.2	0.0	14.7
Mexico	17.3	20.5	34.4	21.4	34.9	16.1	20.1
Paraguay	13.7	19.5	22.4	16.9	22.2	9.2	14.1
Peru	13.3	17.0	19.3	12.8	20.0	12.0	12.0
Uruguay	14.7	20.1	22.9	17.5	23.0	8.7	18.0
Venezuela	12.3	18.0	19.9	13.4	20.0	6.1	14.2
North Africa	**25.9**	**38.4**	**44.1**	**33.8**	**44.5**	**15.6**	**25.4**
Algeria	24.1	35.3	44.5	26.7	45.0	17.7	31.3
Egypt	22.3	42.0	39.7	26.6	40.0	12.1	20.0
Morocco	28.2	38.2	49.6	44.2	50.0	11.3	9.2
Tunisia	28.7	38.0	42.6	37.8	43.0	20.9	36.0
Sub-Saharan Africa	**16.8**	**21.8**	**34.5**	**19.6**	**26.9**	**15.5**	**23.9**
High- and middle-income developing economies[a]	**14.6**	**19.5**	**26.9**	**16.8**	**25.1**	**10.3**	**15.3**
Leading developing economy importers[b]	**9.0**	**11.3**	**17.0**	**9.9**	**18.1**	**7.0**	**11.2**

Source: UNCTAD secretariat calculations, based on UNCTAD and World Bank, *World Integrated Trade Solution* database.

Note: The tariff rates are for the most recent year for which data was available.

    a Argentina, Bolivia, Brazil, Chile, Colombia, Costa Rica, Dominican Republic, Egypt, El Salvador, Indonesia, Malaysia, Mauritius, Mexico, Morocco, Paraguay, Peru, the Philippines, Thailand, Tunisia, Turkey, Uruguay and Venezuela.

    b Brazil, China, Hong Kong (China), Malaysia, Mexico, Republic of Korea, Singapore, Taiwan Province of China, Thailand and Turkey. Classification is based on import data for 1998–1999.

Table 2.3

IMPORT-WEIGHTED MFN AVERAGE TARIFFS OF SELECTED ECONOMIES, BY PRODUCT GROUP

(Per cent)

Importing economy/region	Manufactures (SITC 5–8 less 68)	Textiles (SITC 65)	Clothing (SITC 84)	Leather and travel goods (SITC 611, 612, 831)	Footwear (SITC 85)	Computers and office equipment (SITC 75)	Telecom, audio and video equipment (SITC 76)
Developed countries	**3.1**	**8.1**	**12.2**	**6.9**	**13.0**	**0.1**	**1.7**
Australia	4.7	10.3	21.9	5.1	12.6	0.1	4.5
Canada	3.2	10.0	18.3	5.1	15.1	0.0	0.8
European Union	3.5	8.2	11.7	4.1	11.2	0.1	3.7
Japan	2.2	5.9	11.7	10.3	17.4	0.0	0.0
New Zealand	3.7	3.6	14.2	3.4	10.4	0.1	2.7
United States	3.0	8.1	12.0	8.7	12.8	0.0	0.9
Developing economies							
First-tier NIEs	**1.8**	**1.7**	**1.2**	**0.7**	**0.4**	**0.9**	**1.2**
Hong Kong (China)	0.0	0.0	0.0	0.0	0.0	0.0	0.0
Republic of Korea	6.2	8.6	12.7	6.1	12.9	7.6	8.0
Singapore	0.0	0.0	0.0	0.0	0.0	0.0	0.0
Taiwan Province of China	3.3	5.4	13.2	3.7	6.4	0.4	3.7
ASEAN-4	**6.5**	**14.3**	**22.2**	**7.1**	**21.4**	**1.7**	**6.8**
Indonesia	6.7	11.6	19.2	3.9	18.4	1.8	11.4
Malaysia	5.8	17.7	19.5	7.5	25.4	0.1	6.7
Philippines	3.3	9.7	19.4	8.4	15.0	0.0	2.7
Thailand	10.3	17.4	31.1	9.3	37.4	5.8	11.4
South Asia	**26.7**	**20.5**	**22.3**	**24.6**	**34.7**	**15.7**	**21.7**
Bangladesh	21.7	34.8	..	16.9	..	2.4	17.2
India	31.4	38.3	39.7	27.8	40.0	18.0	28.0
Sri Lanka	5.4	1.0	11.2	13.3	24.1	0.5	3.0
Other Asia	**5.9**	**9.0**	**15.3**	**7.9**	**22.7**	**0.4**	**6.5**
China	5.8	8.9	14.9	7.9	14.9	0.1	6.2
Jordan	19.9	26.3	34.9	35.0	35.0	11.4	32.1
Turkey	5.8	8.6	11.8	7.4	23.5	2.3	6.3
Latin America	**14.1**	**19.0**	**28.3**	**19.3**	**22.8**	**8.5**	**14.9**
Argentina	15.3	20.1	22.8	19.0	33.0	6.9	11.8
Bolivia	9.0	10.0	10.0	10.0	10.0	10.0	10.0
Brazil	15.9	18.9	22.4	14.3	26.6	14.6	16.2
Chile	9.0	9.0	9.0	9.0	9.0	9.0	9.0
Colombia	10.5	17.1	19.5	16.1	20.0	5.0	8.7
Costa Rica	3.9	7.6	13.9	9.0	13.9	0.0	4.1
Dominican Republic	17.8	21.1	27.1	22.0	23.6	10.0	14.1
El Salvador	5.5	14.7	23.9	8.6	20.0	0.0	1.7
Jamaica	10.0	4.1	19.1	17.1	18.6	0.0	5.2
Mexico	14.8	20.3	34.7	21.6	34.9	7.6	17.3
Paraguay	11.7	15.6	21.1	17.3	17.5	5.3	9.1
Peru	12.3	16.6	18.8	12.9	20.0	12.0	12.0
Uruguay	14.4	19.9	22.9	13.4	23.0	4.4	10.2
Venezuela	13.3	17.4	19.8	17.4	20.0	5.4	8.7
North Africa	**22.6**	**38.7**	**44.7**	**38.8**	**44.0**	**7.1**	**11.0**
Algeria	18.7	29.6	44.2	35.0	45.0	6.8	20.8
Egypt	17.6	31.0	38.4	30.0	40.0	9.2	13.3
Morocco	25.3	38.9	50.0	45.0	50.0	4.2	4.8
Tunisia	30.2	41.5	41.5	36.1	43.0	8.2	27.9
Sub-Saharan Africa	**14.7**	**19.1**	**33.1**	**23.5**	**25.9**	**14.7**	**20.3**
High- and middle-income developing economies[a]	**11.6**	**19.9**	**29.9**	**17.1**	**23.7**	**5.4**	**12.5**
Leading developing economy importers[b]	**6.1**	**8.0**	**8.1**	**5.1**	**2.1**	**1.9**	**6.0**

Source: See table 2.2.

Note: The tariff rates are for the most recent year for which data was available.

    a   Argentina, Bolivia, Brazil, Chile, Colombia, Costa Rica, Dominican Republic, Egypt, El Salvador, Indonesia, Malaysia, Mauritius, Mexico, Morocco, Paraguay, Peru, the Philippines, Thailand, Tunisia, Turkey, Uruguay and Venezuela.

    b   Brazil, China, Hong Kong (China), Malaysia, Mexico, Republic of Korea, Singapore, Taiwan Province of China, Thailand and Turkey. Classification is based on import data for 1998–1999.

labour-intensive sectors by the 10 leading developing country importers are substantially lower than those applied by the group of high- and middle-income developing countries, and they are not much higher than those applied by some of the developed countries. Finally, there is no developing country that imposes quota regulations on imports under the WTO Agreement on Textiles and Clothing (ATC). Taken together, the evidence challenges the contention that trade restrictions among developing countries themselves play a central role in the problems associated with the risk of fallacy of composition in traditional labour-intensive manufactures.

As already noted, over the past few years, developing countries have considerably increased their share in world exports of goods from the electronics sector by participating in the labour-intensive segments of international production networks. While simple average tariffs applied by low-income countries are higher than those applied by middle- and high-income developing countries on products from the electronics sector, these tariffs are, with few exceptions, lower in developed than in developing countries, as shown in the last two columns of table 2.2. For a number of reasons, aggregate data on import tariffs are unlikely to reflect fully the market access conditions prevailing in electronics; for instance, trade relationships in these sectors are often based on specific market access regulations or on exchanges between subsidiaries of a multinational enterprise that may enjoy preferential conditions. However, the enterprise-specific evidence required to analyse such trade relationships is unavailable. Nonetheless, the aggregate tariff data suggest that, for both developed and developing countries, market access conditions for the electronics sector are much more favourable than for the traditional labour-intensive manufacturing sector.

The pattern of import-weighted tariffs (table 2.3) is essentially the same as that of simple tariffs.[16] However, the trade-weighted tariffs in the traditional manufacturing sectors applied by developed countries, particularly to textiles and clothing, are in almost all cases higher than simple tariffs, while the opposite holds true for a large number of leading developing economy importers, including the first-tier NIEs, Turkey and a number of Latin American countries such as Argentina, Brazil, Chile and Colombia. As a result, the import-weighted average tariffs on textiles, clothing, leather goods and footwear that are applied by the 10 leading

---

[16] Similar evidence is provided for the more aggregated Multilateral Trade Negotiations' industrial product categories in Bacchetta and Bora (2001).

developing country importers are below those applied by the major developed countries.

2. Preferential trading arrangements and market access

There has been a rapid growth in recent years in the number of preferential trade agreements (PTAs) which discriminate against non-member countries in market access, including in labour-intensive manufactures. A number of such arrangements also involve developing countries. The evidence, however, shows that PTAs among developing countries alone tend to be less restrictive for non-members than those between developed and developing countries. In the latter cases, as described in annex C to chapter 1, developing country members often gain considerable advantage over non-members in access to markets of developed country members in labour-intensive manufactures such as clothing. This alters the distribution of market shares among developing countries, and the outcome is not always favourable to poorer countries. In fact, by allowing more advanced developing countries greater access to markets for labour-intensive manufactures, these arrangements can distort incentives and delay technological upgrading.

The impact of PTAs on trade flows in labour-intensive manufactures depends on the degree of preferences given to members. This can be assessed by the difference between MFN tariffs and effectively applied tariffs; the lower the effectively applied tariffs compared to the MFN tariffs, the higher the trade barriers to non-members. Table 2.4 gives the import-weighted MFN tariffs in the two most prominent PTAs among developing countries (Southern Common Market – MERCOSUR) and the ASEAN Free Trade Area (AFTA). A comparison of the applied tariffs in table 2.4 with the MFN tariffs in table 2.3 shows that among the high- and middle-income member countries of AFTA for which data are available, only in Malaysia are import-weighted preferential tariff rates lower than the import-weighted MFN tariffs, while in MERCOSUR this is true for all countries except Brazil. This is likely to reflect the fact that the AFTA countries generally have significantly lower MFN tariffs than the member countries of MERCOSUR. But it is also noteworthy that the difference between the two tariffs is particularly large for Argentina and Uruguay; in these countries the effectively applied tariffs on most of the traditional labour-intensive manufactures are only half the MFN tariffs.

Table 2.4

EFFECTIVELY APPLIED AVERAGE TARIFFS OF SELECTED COUNTRIES
IN MERCOSUR AND AFTA, BY PRODUCT GROUP

(Per cent)

Importing country	Manufactures (SITC 5–8 less 68)	Textiles (SITC 65)	Clothing (SITC 84)	Leather and travel goods (SITC 611, 612, 831)	Footwear (SITC 85)
MERCOSUR					
Argentina	11.8	11.6	15.7	15.3	11.9
Brazil	15.2	18.9	22.4	15.2	26.6
Paraguay	10.8	14.1	16.4	16.6	17.2
Uruguay	8.1	11.6	12.5	4.5	12.2
AFTA					
Indonesia	5.8	11.2	19.1	3.1	17.3
Malaysia	5.5	16.1	16.7	6.7	23.5
Philippines	2.9	10.8	17.6	8.0	15.0
Singapore	0.0	0.0	0.0	0.0	0.0
Thailand	10.3	17.4	31.1	9.3	37.4

Source: See table 2.2.
Note: The tariff rates are for the most recent year for which data was available.

Clearly, tariff differentiation between members and non-members is
expected to favour imports from member countries at the expense of non-
members. However, such arrangements do not simply divert trade; they
may also create trade if they help accelerate growth. As can be seen in
table 2.5, trade within MERCOSUR and AFTA has been growing much
faster than imports from non-members, both in aggregate and for selected
labour-intensive manufactures (table 2.5). During the period 1990–1999,
total intraregional imports increased on average by about 16 per cent a
year in MERCOSUR and by 11 per cent in AFTA, while extraregional
imports increased by about 12 per cent for MERCOSUR and by about
6 per cent for AFTA. However, in MERCOSUR growth of imports from
non-members substantially exceeded the average rate of growth of world
imports (6 per cent), while in AFTA it kept pace with the growth in world
imports. In MERCOSUR, imports of labour-intensive manufactures, both
from members and non-members, grew faster than world imports in
almost all product categories listed in table 2.5. In AFTA, imports from
members grew faster than world imports in all sectors except footwear
and telecommunications equipment, while the rate of growth in imports
from non-members exceeded that in world imports only in clothing and

Table 2.5

INTRAREGIONAL IMPORTS OF MERCOSUR AND AFTA, 1980–1999

(Per cent)

	Share in total imports			Growth rate		Memo item: Growth rate of extraregional imports	
	1990	1995	1999	1980– 1989	1990– 1999	1980– 1989	1990– 1999
MERCOSUR							
All products	14.5	18.1	19.1	13.0	15.7	10.2	11.5
Manufactures	12.0	13.9	15.1	10.9	18.6	6.9	15.2
Textiles	29.8	25.2	30.6	10.5	18.5	-1.8	18.0
Clothing	52.1	21.8	27.8	4.8	15.7	-20.3	29.8
Footwear	12.1	23.3	51.2	-1.5	45.5	-9.3	16.1
Leather goods	63.1	49.0	46.3	74.3	1.2	24.3	9.2
Computers and office equipment	2.0	1.7	5.8	-2.5	33.5	9.5	18.1
Telecom, audio and video equipment	3.1	2.7	5.0	-1.4	24.1	2.8	17.4
AFTA							
All products	15.1	17.1	21.2	8.7	10.7	7.9	5.8
Manufactures	11.8	15.8	21.3	20.0	14.6	10.2	6.0
Textiles	8.0	10.6	13.9	12.0	7.2	10.8	0.1
Clothing	53.8	48.9	51.5	24.0	6.6	13.3	7.7
Footwear	30.5	26.6	29.7	17.8	3.2	11.2	3.6
Leather goods	4.9	5.9	8.5	13.0	10.3	19.8	3.2
Computers and office equipment	24.8	37.6	37.1	75.0	19.9	27.6	12.4
Telecom, audio and video equipment	30.0	30.1	28.1	34.2	3.1	12.2	4.2
Memo item:							
WORLD							
All products	.	.	.	6.7	5.9	.	.
Manufactures	.	.	.	10.2	6.9	.	.
Textiles	.	.	.	8.2	3.5	.	.
Clothing	.	.	.	11.2	6.2	.	.
Footwear	.	.	.	8.9	5.0	.	.
Leather goods	.	.	.	12.4	5.7	.	.
Computers and office equipment	.	.	.	17.8	11.2	.	.
Telecom, audio and video equipment	.	.	.	13.0	9.8	.	.

Source: UNCTAD secretariat calculations, based on UN/DESA, *Commodity Trade Statistics* database.

office machines. Therefore, on this measure, the evidence suggests that, despite tariff differentiation, these fast growing PTAs have not had negative effects on total trade with non-members.[17] This result also holds true for trade in labour-intensive manufactures, although the evidence is more varied for AFTA. Consequently, it gives further support to the

---

[17] It is difficult to judge the counterfactual (i.e. how much the trade of the members of these PTAs would have grown with non-members) in the absence of such arrangements. Yeats (1998) believes that there was trade diversion in MERCOSUR.

argument (cited earlier) challenging the contention that trade restrictions among developing countries themselves have been a key reason for fallacy of composition in the traditional labour-intensive manufacturing sectors.

By contrast, preferential market access provided to developing countries in PTAs between developed and developing countries appears to have a much greater impact on the distribution of market shares in traditional labour-intensive manufactures. Table 2.6 shows that import-weighted effectively applied tariffs by the EU and the United States on clothing and footwear imported from their respective partners in PTAs are lower than they are for those imported from non-member developing countries, and that they are significantly lower than MFN tariffs. This explains why the shares of North African and Eastern European countries and Turkey in clothing imports of the EU have grown considerably over the past decade compared to countries which are known to have a competitive edge in these products. Even for such a strong competitor as China, growth in exports lagged, on average, behind that of countries with preferential market access. It is also notable that the performance of the Eastern European countries and Turkey is much less impressive in the United States market, where they do not benefit from the same preferential treatment. Similarly, by virtue of its membership of NAFTA, Mexico's performance in the United States clothing market is much more impressive than that of other developing country exporters and that of its own exports in the EU market. A similar pattern applies to footwear imports by the EU and the United States from their respective trading partners.

F. Policy responses

Although the preceding analysis shows a complex and nuanced picture, there is enough evidence that there might be a risk of excessive competition among developing countries in world markets for labour-intensive products and for FDI through participation in the labour-intensive segments of international production networks. This could disrupt the development process by causing significant terms-of-trade losses and create frictions in the global trading system. To what extent such potential problems can be avoided will depend on three sets of factors:

- First, on faster growth of markets for labour-intensive manufactures in more advanced economies – both the industrialized countries and

Table 2.6

CLOTHING AND FOOTWEAR IMPORTS OF THE EUROPEAN UNION AND THE UNITED STATES
AND RELATED IMPORT-WEIGHTED TARIFFS, BY REGION, 1990–1999

(Per cent)

	Clothing					Footwear				
	Tariffs		Import shares			Tariffs		Import shares		
	MFN	Effectively applied	1990	1995	2000	MFN	Effectively applied	1990	1995	2000
	2000		1990	1995	2000	2000		1990	1995	2000
Imports of the European Union from										
Countries with preferential market access[a]										
North Africa	12.2	0.0	4.9	6.8	7.2	8.3	0.0	0.6	1.5	1.8
Eastern Europe	12.2	0.0	3.6	9.9	10.9	9.5	0.0	2.6	6.0	7.5
Turkey	12.0	0.0	5.4	6.7	7.4	10.4	0.0	0.1	0.2	0.1
Other economies										
China	11.1	9.2	5.1	7.7	10.6	12.4	8.7	2.8	7.6	11.1
India	10.8	9.0	2.8	3.9	3.4	8.2	5.7	1.0	1.3	1.6
Mexico	9.9	6.0	0.0	0.0	0.0	8.6	4.5	0.2	0.1	0.1
NIEs	11.9	11.9	11.1	8.1	8.6	11.3	11.2	11.5	4.7	3.9
ASEAN-4	10.8	8.9	4.2	4.8	5.5	11.6	8.1	4.9	9.6	7.6
Imports of the United States from										
Countries with preferential market access										
Mexico	12.9	0.8	2.6	7.0	13.1	11.2	3.9	1.2	1.4	1.9
Other economies										
China	9.3	9.3	13.6	14.9	13.3	14.4	14.4	16.1	49.7	62.9
India	11.5	11.3	2.6	3.3	3.2	7.3	7.3	0.5	0.7	0.8
North Africa	11.8	11.8	0.4	0.7	0.8	7.5	7.5	0.0	0.0	0.0
Eastern Europe	13.1	13.0	0.5	0.7	0.6	7.3	7.3	0.7	0.9	0.8
NIEs	12.6	12.6	40.6	22.2	15.0	14.2	14.2	44.8	8.1	2.0
ASEAN-4	11.8	11.6	11.2	13.6	12.1	13.2	13.2	6.0	12.5	7.5
Turkey	11.5	11.4	1.3	1.7	1.7	13.5	13.5	0.0	0.0	0.0

Source: UNCTAD secretariat calculations, based on UNCTAD and World Bank, *World Integrated Trade Solution* database and UN/DESA, *Commodity Trade Statistics* database.
Note: *Eastern Europe* includes: Bulgaria, Czech Republic (1995 and 2000), Czechoslovakia (1990), Estonia (1995 and 2000), Hungary, Latvia (1995 and 2000), Lithuania (1995 and 2000), Poland, Romania, Slovakia (1995 and 2000) and Slovenia (1995 and 2000). *North Africa* includes: Egypt, Morocco and Tunisia. *NIEs* include: Hong Kong (China), Republic of Korea, Singapore and Taiwan Province of China. *ASEAN-4* includes: Indonesia, Malaysia, the Philippines and Thailand.
  a For the types of preferential trade agreements, see WTO (2000).

the first-tier NIEs – which in turn depends on faster income growth
as well as improved market access;

• Second, on how quickly the middle-income countries are able to
   move out of labour-intensive manufactures and create space for
   lower-income countries, both in the markets of advanced industrial
   countries and in their own markets; and

- Finally, emphasizing expansion of developing countries' domestic markets for overcoming their deep-seated problems of unemployment and poverty.

Regarding potential markets in industrial countries, it was estimated in *TDR 1999* that by the year 2005 developing countries would be able to earn an additional $700 billion from annual exports of a number of low-technology, labour-intensive products if protectionist barriers were dismantled. This amounts to about 35 per cent of the total export earnings or 60 per cent of earnings from manufactured exports that the developing countries registered at the beginning of 2000. However, as discussed above, recent developments in trade policies in industrial countries show that there are difficulties in the easing of restrictions in such sectors.

In particular, there are concerns over the implementation of the ATC; simulations on the sectoral impact of the removal of quotas in the importing countries lead some to believe that the safeguards included in that agreement to prevent "serious damage" to domestic industry might be invoked by countries in North America and the EU to delay the removal of remaining quotas (Walmsley and Hertel, 2001). But even if trade in textiles and clothing were to be brought fully under WTO rules, it could still be impeded by relatively high tariffs and tariff escalation in the main developed country importers.

The mounting pressure in industrialized countries to raise the level of protection in trade stems from the coincidence of high unemployment levels and growing wage inequality in these countries with sharp increases in labour-intensive manufactured imports from developing countries. While there is little doubt that rapid trade liberalization and surges in imports can cause dislocations in the labour market, the link between trade and employment in the industrialized countries cannot be considered independently of their overall macroeconomic conditions and labour market policies.[18] As discussed in greater detail in *TDR 1995* (Part Two, chap. II), labour market problems in these countries are rooted in slow and erratic growth and a reluctance to undertake the structural reforms needed to adjust to sectoral dislocations brought about by greater integration into the multilateral trading system (see also UNCTAD, 2001a).

---

[18] For a discussion of such dislocations due to the relocation of low-skill jobs to developing countries, see Feenstra and Hanson (2001).

It is notable that the export performance of the NIEs (which account for two thirds of the increase in import penetration of manufactures by the developing countries) has not been without precedent in the past 50 years. For example, between 1958 and 1975 penetration of goods from both Japan and Italy into the United States market and the national markets of what were the other five members of the then European Economic Community (EEC) was on a scale comparable to the rise of today's late industrializers. Neither in Europe nor in the United States were these developments associated with labour market problems of the kind experienced in the past two decades; rather, the increasing flow of manufactures from Italy to its EEC partners was accompanied by a large migration of labour in the same direction to meet labour shortages. Thus a return to rapid and sustained growth and full employment policies in the industrialized countries is crucial for averting problems associated with fallacy of composition and potential frictions within the multilateral trading system.

The growth in trade among developing countries noted in the previous chapter also opens new opportunities for avoiding difficulties in markets for labour-intensive products. In particular, industrial upgrading in more advanced developing countries would allow new players to take over labour-intensive activities in line with the "flying geese paradigm" (*TDR 1996*, Part Two, chap. I); this would open up space for them in their own markets as well as in the markets of the more advanced economies. This has already happened to a certain extent: China and the other highly populated, low-income countries that have adopted more export-oriented strategies gained much of the market shares given up by the first-tier NIEs when these economies shifted to more capital- and technology-intensive exports. However, because of the failure to undertake timely industrial upgrading, some exporters from the middle-income countries in Latin America and the second-tier NIEs appear to have been negatively affected. Their problems can be aggravated if highly populated countries such as China and India rapidly expand their exports in labour-intensive manufactures. As already noted, upgrading in many of these countries, notably Mexico and the second-tier NIEs, should include the objective of replacing imported components and parts with domestically produced ones, as well as increased reliance on domestic markets (*TDR 2000*: 68–71).

Certainly, the industrial upgrading needed in the middle-income countries depends, to a large extent, on the policies they pursue in such areas as trade, industry and technology; the kinds of policies adopted by the first-tier NIEs for this purpose and the options available are well known.[19] While multilateral trade agreements have restricted the ability to employ some national policies involving support and protection for industries, there is still some policy space for upgrading by the middle-income countries, particularly if this set of issues is kept in mind in the forthcoming multilateral trade negotiations in the WTO.

The outcome will also depend on the extent to which large economies such as China, India and Indonesia will rely on foreign markets to create jobs and incomes for large segments of their population. It is true that growth of manufacturing and industrialization in the first-tier NIEs depended heavily on expansion of exports, particularly at the early stages of their development. However, these countries were poor in natural resources, and this necessitated a rapid move into labour-intensive manufacturing to earn the foreign exchange needed for imports of capital goods and some essential primary commodities such as oil. Moreover, their small size – collectively their population is smaller than that of Guangdong province in China – and hence small domestic market, meant that their industries needed to seek markets abroad in order to achieve the necessary economies of scale in production. Indeed, historical evidence demonstrates, in general, an inverse relationship between trade orientation and economic size; among countries with similar levels of per capita income, the ratio of trade to income tends to be lower in countries with larger populations.

This means that countries such as China and India can rely less on foreign markets for their industrialization than did the first-tier NIEs in their earlier stages of industrialization. Indeed, as discussed in the subsequent chapter, for China greater reliance on domestic sources of growth may prove to be a more viable strategy than maintaining the recent momentum in labour-intensive manufactured exports. Its skill mix and endowments are sufficiently well developed to allow rapid upgrading in a number of technology-intensive sectors to enable it to earn the foreign exchange needed for continued growth in economic activity. This is also true for India. Such a strategy would also provide greater space for smaller newcomers in labour-intensive manufactures.

A strengthening of regional economic ties could help this process along in East and South Asia and South America. Conventional economic thinking tends to dismiss regional arrangements as a second-best solution

---

[19] For a recent synthesis of these policies and the debate over whether they are replicable under current global conditions and constraints, see UNCTAD (2002).

for meeting development goals, and as a potential stumbling-block on the road to a fully open and integrated multilateral system. However, this conclusion is based on a somewhat utopian view of the global economy. Where domestic firms still have weak technological and productive capacities and the global economic context is characterized by systemic biases and asymmetries, regional arrangements may well provide the most supportive environment in which to pursue national development strategies. The fact that many of the rapidly growing economies are in East Asia suggests that the regional dimension played an important role in their industrialization.

As described in detail in *TDR 1996*, the successful use of strategic trade and industrial policies, as well as various macroeconomic pressures originating in the region's more advanced economies, led to a pattern of regional division of labour, described as the "flying geese" model. As the leading economies in the region successfully shifted from resource-based and labour-intensive industries to increasingly sophisticated manufacturing activities, they provided space for the less developed countries to enter simpler manufacturing stages. Regional trade and investment flows played a central role in this process by helping to create markets and by the transfer of skills and technology to neighbouring countries (Rowthorn, 1996). This sustainable growth process needs to combine market forces with targeted industrial policies. The challenge now lies in the extension of this regional dynamic to include newly emerging countries such as China and India, as well as other less developed countries in South and East Asia. Although experiences with regional arrangements among developing countries elsewhere have proved less satisfactory, the question remains whether they could, nonetheless, emulate the kind of growth pattern that was established in East Asia.

Since regional economic arrangements imply close interdependence among a group of economies, there is the risk that problems in one country may be transmitted to its neighbours. Arguably, that danger has intensified in today's globalizing world. In fact, a number of changes in the regional pattern of integration during the 1990s do appear to have contributed to the instability which hit East Asia towards the end of the 1990s. With volatile capital flows fuelling a boom-bust cycle, a more fragile macroeconomic context has developed which is vulnerable to shifting investor sentiment. Thus a return to stable and rapid regional growth needs to be underpinned not only by policies directed at the upgrading of production and exports, but also, in view of the close links between trade and finance, by accompanying regional arrangements to ensure the stability of financial markets, including lending facilities and agreement on a sustainable pattern of exchange rates (*TDR 2001*, chap. V).

Finally, as argued in *TDR 1996*, avoiding potential pitfalls in formulating and implementing an export strategy requires constant monitoring of developments in markets for various manufactured products, projecting the possible evolution of global supply and demand conditions. This task can best be accomplished by an international agency such as UNCTAD. In this study, an attempt is made to identify the developments in world trade in manufactures over the past two decades, the extent of participation of developing countries in dynamic, high value-added products, and the degree of competition building up in labour-intensive manufactures. To help developing countries in the formulation of their trade strategies and to provide early warning signals, the analysis of dynamic products will need to be updated on a regular basis. It will also need to be extended to include information on and analysis of trends in the prices of labour-intensive manufactures, which now constitute the bulk of exports from developing countries.

References

Akiyama T and Larson DF (1994). The adding-up problem. Strategies for primary commodity exports in sub-Saharan Africa. Policy Research Working Paper, 1245. Washington, DC, World Bank, January.

Athukorala P (1993). Manufactured exports from developing countries and their terms of trade: A re-examination of the Sarkar-Singer results. *World Development*, 21: 1607–1613.

Bacchetta M and Bora B (2001). Post-Uruguay Round market access barriers for industrial products. Policy Issues in International Trade and Commodities Study Series, 12 (UNCTAD/ITCD/TAB/13). United Nations publication, sales no. E.01.II.D.23, New York and Geneva.

Barro RJ and Lee JW (2000). International data on educational attainment: Updates and implications. Working Paper 42. Cambridge, MA, Harvard University, Center for International Development.

Berge K and Crowe T (1997). The terms of trade facing South Korea with respect to its trade with LDCs and DMEs. Working Paper, 12. Oxford, University of Oxford, Queen Elisabeth House, August.

Bhagwati J (1958). Immiserizing growth: A geometrical note. *The Review of Economic Studies*, XXV(3), June.

Bleaney MF (1993). Liberalisation and the terms of trade of developing countries: A cause for concern? *The World Economy*, 16: 453–466.

Cline WR (1982). Can the East Asian model of development be generalized? *World Development*, 10(2): 81–90.

Feenstra RC and Hanson GH (2001). Global production sharing and rising inequality: A survey of trade and wages. NBER Working Paper, 8372. Cambridge, MA, National Bureau of Economic Research, July.

Havrylyshyn O (1990). Penetrating the fallacy of export composition. In: Singer H, Hatti N and Tandon T, eds. *North-South Trade in Manufactures*. New Delhi, Indus Publishing Co.

Hoekman B, Ng F and Olarreaga M (2001). Eliminating excessive tariffs on exports of least developed countries. Working Paper, 2604. Washington, DC, World Bank, May.

Ianchovichina E, Martin W and Fukase E (2000). Assessing the implications of merchandise trade liberalization in China's accession to WTO. Paper presented to the Roundtable on China's Accession to the WTO sponsored by the Chinese Economic Society and the World Bank, 8 July, Pundong, Shanghai. Washington, DC, World Bank, June.

Maizels A (2000). The manufactures terms of trade of developing countries with the United States, 1981–97. Working Paper, 36. Oxford, Oxford University, Queen Elisabeth House, January.

Maizels A, Palaskas TB and Crowe T (1998). The Prebisch Singer hypothesis revisited. In: Sapsford D and Chen J, eds. *Development Economics and Policy*. London and Basingstoke, Macmillan.

Martin W (1993). The fallacy of composition and developing country exports of manufactures. *The World Economy*, 16(2): 159–172.

Michalopoulos C (1999). Trade policy and market access issues for developing countries: Implications for the Millennium Round. Working Paper, 2214. Washington, DC, World Bank.

Minford P, Riley J and Nowell E (1997). Trade, technology and labour markets in the world economy, 1970–90: A computable general equilibrium analysis. *Journal of Development Studies*, 34 (2): 1–34.

OECD (1999). *Post-Uruguay Round Tariff Regimes: Achievements and Outlook*. Paris, Organisation for Economic Co-operation and Development.

Rowthorn R (1996). East Asian development: The flying paradigm reconsidered. In: UNCTAD, *East Asian Development: Lessons for a New Global Environment*, Study No. 10. Geneva.

Rowthorn R (1997). Replicating the experience of the newly industrialising economies. Working Paper, 57. Cambridge, UK, Cambridge University, Economic and Social Research Council, Centre for Business Studies.

Sarkar P and Singer HW (1991). Manufactured exports of developing countries and their terms of trade since 1965. *World Development*, 19: 333–340.

Singer HW (1975).The distribution of gains revisited. In: Cairncross A and Puri M, eds. *The Strategy of International Development. Essays in the Economics of Backwardness*. London and Basingstoke, Macmillan.

UNCTAD (2001a). Globalization and the labour market. Paper prepared by the UNCTAD secretariat for the ILO Working Party on the Social Dimension of Globalization (UNCTAD/GDS/MDPB/Misc.14), Geneva, 12 November.

UNCTAD (2001b). *Improving Market Access for Least Developed Countries* (UNCTAD/DITC/TNCD/4). Geneva, May.

UNCTAD (2002). Development strategies in a globalizing world. Mimeo. Geneva, January.

UNCTAD/Commonwealth Secretariat (2001). Duty and quota free market access for LDCs: An analysis of Quad initiatives (UNCTAD/DITC/TAB/Misc.7). Joint Study. London and Geneva. July.

UNCTAD/WTO (2000). The post-Uruguay Round tariff environment for developing countries' exports: Tariff peaks and tariff escalation. Joint Study (TD/B/COM.1/14/Rev.1). Geneva, UNCTAD/World Trade Organization, January.

UNDP (2001). *Human Development Report 2001*. United Nations publication, sales no. E.99.III.B. New York.

Walmsley TL and Hertel TW (2001). China's accession to the WTO: Timing is everything. *The World Economy*, 24: 1019–1049.

Wood A (1994). *North-South Trade, Employment and Inequality*. Oxford, Clarendon Press.

World Bank (1996). *Global Economic Prospects and the Developing Countries*. Washington, DC.

WTO (2000). *Trade Policy Review: European Union*, 1:31, Geneva, World Trade Organization.

WTO (2001). *Market Access: Unfinished Business. Post-Uruguay Round Inventory and Issues*. Special Studies, 6. Geneva, World Trade Organization.

Yeats A (1998). Does MERCOSUR's trade performance justify concerns about the effects of regional trade agreements? *World Bank Economic Review*, 12: 1–28.

Zheng Z and Yumin Z (2002). China's terms of trade in manufactures, 1993–2000. UNCTAD Discussion Paper No. 161. June. Geneva.

Chapter 3

CHINA'S ACCESSION TO WTO:
MANAGING INTEGRATION AND INDUSTRIALIZATION

A. Introduction

In *TDR 1999* the analysis of trade and growth in the developing world (Part Two, chap. IV) – prepared at a time when China's bilateral negotiations for accession to the World Trade Organization (WTO) were well under way – noted that, unlike other developing countries, China had managed to improve both its trade and growth performance over the past two decades. Many developing countries, particularly those which had resorted to big bang liberalization of trade and the capital account, experienced a simultaneous worsening of their external trade balances and declines in their economic growth rates. China, on the other hand, together with some smaller economies, bucked the general trend, expanding exports faster than imports and accelerating growth without relying on foreign savings. On the eve of its accession to the WTO,[1] China's trade in both goods and services had been growing at double digit rates (more than twice the world average) for over a decade; it now accounts for almost 4 per cent of world merchandise exports and 3.5 per cent of imports.[2]

This strong trade performance has been associated with a growth in the share of manufactures, mostly labour-intensive, which amounts to 90 per cent of China's total exports. China has also been increasingly involved in assembly of technology-intensive products: exports of telecommunications equipment and computers now account for a quarter of its total exports. A number of Chinese exports, including travel goods, toys, sporting goods, footwear and non-textile clothing, account for over 20 per cent of total world exports of these products. Raw materials and intermediate and capital goods (including machinery and equipment, chemicals, ores and metals) constitute the major share of China's imports, while the share of consumer goods is relatively small. China's main export markets are the leading industrialized countries, but it has also

---

[1] China became a member of the WTO in December 2001.
[2] In this chapter, the data on China do not include those for Hong Kong Special Administrative Region (Hong Kong, China), Macao Special Administrative Region (Macao, China) and Taiwan Province of China, unless otherwise specified.

been strengthening its regional trade links, notably with the East Asian newly industrializing economies (NIEs). Its trade surplus with the United States now exceeds that of Japan with the United States, and it also runs surpluses with Japan and the European Union (EU) in merchandise trade (table 3.3 below).

The accession of China to the WTO has raised the issue of the possible impact of the adoption of multilateral trade disciplines on its trade performance and on that of its trading partners. For China, accession implies, above all, liberalization and the opening up of its markets to greater foreign competition. For its trading partners, given the demographic and economic size of China, its accession to the WTO implies a significant change in the trading environment that will affect countries in different ways. For some, it presents an opportunity to pursue or expand their commercial interests in China's vast and growing market under the protection of multilateral rules and procedures, while others take a more cautious approach, emphasizing the added competition that will arise with China's accession. Perhaps the more important issue for developing countries is the extent to which China's accession could influence the trends discussed in the previous chapters, including the risk of a fallacy of composition.

Much has already been written on the possible implications of China's accession to the WTO, and some quantitative projections have been made for China and its trading partners. However, it is difficult to predict with any reasonable degree of accuracy the extent to which accession will change China's economic performance from the path it would have followed had it remained out of the WTO. This is not only because of the difficulty in determining the counterfactual but, more importantly, because the impact of accession will depend on how the agreements reached will be interpreted and implemented, and on the policy response of China and its trading partners to future economic developments resulting from accession. Hence, the purpose of this chapter is not to predict what may or may not happen to China or its trading partners, but to discuss the issues raised by China's accession in terms of the questions analyzed in this study.

In order to place these issues in the broader context of historical experience, it is useful to analyze how the trade liberalization implicit in the conditions of China's accession to the WTO compares with the big bang liberalization pursued by a number of developing countries.[3] It should first be noted that China's liberalization in the context of its accession is part of a negotiated package involving certain long-term benefits and concessions from its trading partners. These include, in particular, the granting of a Permanent Normal Trade Relations status with its largest trading partner, the United States, and the eventual elimination of discriminatory, WTO-inconsistent, measures against China's exports within an agreed time frame.

Second, a comparison can be made in terms of the pace of liberalization. The bulk of China's liberalization is due to take place in the years immediately following its accession to the WTO – and the market-opening commitments made by China are sweeping. They will profoundly affect the protected sectors of the economy in agriculture, industry and services. However, China's post-accession liberalization, especially with regard to its imports, actually constitutes part of an ongoing process that already started over a decade ago. Pre-accession tariff and non-tariff measures (NTMs) in China have not been high by the standards of some other developing countries that have been pursuing import substitution strategies over the past few years. And the terms of accession allow phasing-out periods in a number of areas. In addition, the export drive that has so far dominated Chinese commercial policies has involved considerable liberalization of sectors that are directly linked to foreign markets, particularly where foreign-funded enterprises (FFEs) are involved.[4]

Third, China is not liberalizing out of failure. This is a major difference between China and other developing countries, where the decision to liberalize was prompted by their failure to establish competitive industries behind high barriers, and the expectation that closer integration into the trading system, by ensuring steadily rising export earnings, would prevent recurrent balance-of-payments crises and stop-go development. Liberalization in China is occurring during a period

---

[3] For a description and assessment of these experiences, see Agosin and Tussie (1993). See also *TDR 1999* (Part Two, chap. IV, and annex to chap. IV).
[4] FFEs include equity joint ventures, contractual joint ventures, wholly foreign-owned enterprises and joint exploration companies for special extraction industries. They range from large transnational corporations to small and medium-sized enterprises owned mainly by investors of Chinese ethnic origin from East Asia.

of extremely successful export expansion in manufacturing that is associated with a sound and sustained balance-of-payments position and a large stock of international reserves. Thus it is not designed to overcome a foreign exchange constraint. In this sense, it resembles more closely those economies that successfully liberalized their trade regimes, such as the Republic of Korea and Taiwan Province of China in the 1970s and 1980s (Agosin and Tussie, 1993: 28–29).

However, this does not mean that China is immune to the kind of difficulties experienced by countries that shifted rapidly from import substitution to outward orientation. The Chinese economy has a dualistic industrial structure. While it has a highly competitive labour-intensive, export-oriented manufacturing sector dominated by FFEs, it also has a fairly traditional capital-intensive industrial sector dominated by State-owned enterprises (SOEs), as well as an agricultural sector that enjoys a relatively high degree of government support and protection. Although the SOEs account for about half of China's exports, their sales are, on balance, directed primarily at domestic markets. The SOE sector has been undergoing transformation and restructuring for several years, but the reform process is far from complete. Thus a rapid dismantling of trade barriers and removal of subsidies could expose SOEs to foreign competition, which could undermine their export performance, as well as lead to a surge in imports. This may create problems not so much for the balance of payments – as has often been the case in countries with weak export bases – but for employment and living standards of workers employed by SOEs. Yet a rapid redeployment of labour to more competitive export-oriented, labour-intensive manufacturing is probably not feasible; nor is it advisable since it could flood the markets in these products and provoke contingency protection measures by China's trading partners through various mechanisms, such as transitional product-specific safeguards which are included among the conditions of accession agreed by China. Although a number of domestic policy instruments may be deployed to defend jobs so as to allow more gradual reform, problems of adjustment can be expected to arise in the short and medium term in sectors dominated by SOEs.

Finally, it is generally agreed that the impact of trade liberalization depends on how the exchange rate is managed, and in this respect China is better placed than many developing countries. To prevent payments difficulties and serious dislocations, it is often recommended that import liberalization be accompanied by currency devaluation. However, in a number of developing countries import liberalization was combined with liberalization of the capital account, which, in many instances, initially encouraged short-term, liquid capital inflows. While these inflows facilitated the financing of their growing trade deficits, they also exerted upward pressure on the exchange rate, thereby weakening competitiveness and export performance, and leading eventually to payments difficulties and financial crises. China, on the other hand, has a strong payments position and large inflows of foreign direct investment (FDI), and is therefore unlikely to experience payments difficulties, even in the event of a sharp surge in imports. This, together with its existing more restrictive capital-account regime,[5] should allow China to manage its exchange rate, maintaining a tight grip on its currency, its capital flows and finances generally, in order to facilitate adjustment during the initial post-accession period.

How China will handle these problems will affect the outcome, not only for China itself but also for its trading partners. The analysis in the previous chapter suggests that trade liberalization in China may result in a surge in imports of certain resource-based products and those with high technology intensity, which will benefit countries that have a competitive edge in the manufacture of these products for export. On the other hand, it may improve the trading opportunities of Chinese enterprises by facilitating their entry into new markets. More importantly, accession can make China an even more attractive location for foreign firms, and this could lead to greater competition among developing countries for FDI linked to the labour-intensive segments of international production networks. There are already signs that China has been attracting large inflows of FDI – including from economies in East Asia – seeking low-cost locations for exports to third markets; furthermore, many transnational corporations (TNCs) are seeking to establish a commercial presence there. To the extent that such inflows divert investment from other developing countries, this can intensify competition among them to attract FDI. The outcome for China and other developing countries will also depend on the nature of inflows of FDI, and hence on the policy approach adopted by China and its competitors as well as foreign firms.

B. Accession: changes in China's import regime

1. Tariff and non-tariff measures (NTMs)

China had already reduced its tariffs significantly before its accession to the WTO. Both its simple and weighted tariff rates were more than halved between 1993 and 1998 (Ianchovichina and Martin, 2001, table

---

[5] For a description of China's capital-account regime, see Ge (2001).

5). The effective tariff rate, as measured by the ratio of tariffs to total imports, stood at 4.5 in the first half of 1999 (JP Morgan, 1999: 6), and there were further cuts at the beginning of 2001. Most of these cuts were related to parts and components for processing in the manufacturing sector, with hardly any change in the weighted average tariffs on primary products, particularly agricultural commodities. Before accession, imported inputs by FFEs were generally exempted from tariffs, but most finished manufactured goods were subject to duties, which, in some cases, were quite heavy.

Table 3.1 provides data on weighted average tariff rates for 2001 and the agreed Chinese bound tariff rates reported in the Protocol of Accession, to be implemented over a 10-year period starting from the date of accession. The products are ranked according to percentage changes in bound tariff offers in relation to figures for 2001. The decline in China's average weighted tariff rate between the time of its accession and the final year, from 13.7 per cent to 5.7 per cent, is quite significant, since it represents cuts over and above those already made.[6] The table also indicates that heavily protected items are among those most affected by tariff cuts, including wheat, rice, plant fibres (cotton), sugar and vegetable oils among agricultural goods, and beverages and tobacco, motor vehicles and parts, clothing and textiles. Further, China has also made commitments to eliminate NTMs, particularly those relating to agricultural products, which at present face high NTMs.

It should be noted that while the period of phased reduction extends to 2005 and beyond, the bulk of the reductions in tariffs and NTMs is to take place soon after accession, and indeed some cases even upon accession. During the first two years, tariffs on most agricultural and manufactured goods will be reduced, particularly on a number of highly protected agricultural products, motor vehicles and labour-intensive manufactures. NTMs on 162 out of 377 items will be eliminated upon accession and another 75 within two years, and all import licences will be eliminated upon accession.

2. Subsidies

The pressure on import-competing sectors will arise not only from the reduction in trade barriers, but also, perhaps more importantly, from

---

[6] According to a World Bank estimate, the weighted tariff rate will fall from 18.7 per cent in 1998 to 7.85 per cent in 2005 (Ianchovichina and Martin, 2001, tables 2 and 4).

Table 3.1

POST-ACCESSION REDUCTION IN WEIGHTED TARIFF RATES FOR CHINA'S MAIN IMPORTS[a]

Product group	Tariff rate 2001 (MFN)	final[b] (bound)	Tariff reduction (per cent) after one year	two years	five years	final year[b]
Cereal grains	91.1	3.0	96.7	96.7	96.7	96.7
Oil seeds	96.9	3.9	96.0	96.0	96.0	96.0
Beverages and tobacco products	57.8	10.4	65.7	74.2	81.9	81.9
Electronic equipment	10.6	2.3	70.9	76.9	78.3	78.3
Vegetable oils and fats	39.3	10.2	50.2	58.3	74.0	74.0
Wood products	10.0	3.4	42.7	54.1	66.0	66.0
Paper products, publishing	9.3	3.3	39.3	51.7	64.2	64.2
Crops	21.7	8.4	32.5	46.8	61.2	61.2
Textiles	20.5	8.7	22.9	36.4	57.4	57.4
Plant-based fibres	84.3	37.7	39.4	47.4	55.3	55.3
Motor vehicles and parts	31.3	14.1	31.0	39.4	54.9	55.0
Dairy products	19.0	8.9	29.2	38.0	53.1	53.1
Vegetables, fruit, nuts	25.9	12.6	29.1	39.9	51.1	51.1
Machinery and equipment	13.4	6.6	37.0	45.7	50.7	50.7
Meat products	18.6	9.9	28.0	37.3	46.7	46.7
Sugar	77.9	43.8	27.3	35.5	43.8	43.8
Processed rice	114.0	65.0	43.0	43.0	43.0	43.0
Paddy rice	114.0	65.0	43.0	43.0	43.0	43.0
Wheat	114.0	65.0	37.7	40.4	43.0	43.0
Ferrous metals	9.1	5.2	37.5	40.5	42.8	42.8
Chemical, rubber, plastic products	14.1	8.1	22.2	27.6	38.0	42.8
Forestry	2.3	1.3	42.5	42.5	42.5	42.5
Food products	16.8	9.8	25.7	34.5	41.6	41.7
Fishing	14.2	8.5	21.0	31.0	40.2	40.2
Metals	7.0	4.2	35.7	37.9	39.5	39.5
Wearing apparel	23.8	14.9	10.8	20.4	37.3	37.3
Leather products	11.6	8.0	26.7	28.9	31.4	31.4
Meat	14.1	9.9	17.4	23.6	29.9	29.9
Transport equipment	5.0	3.6	21.2	25.0	28.4	28.4
Metal products	9.7	7.4	17.8	21.2	23.6	23.6
Mineral products	14.4	11.4	15.8	18.2	20.6	20.6
Petroleum, coal products	8.4	6.7	19.8	19.8	19.8	19.8
Manufactures	19.5	15.8	7.2	11.9	19.0	19.0
Animal products	9.4	8.0	9.3	11.9	14.5	14.5
Average of above	14.6	6.1	40.5	47.2	54.3	58.3
All goods	13.7	5.7	41.6	48.0	54.9	58.8

Source: UNCTAD, *Trade Analysis and Information System* (TRAINS) database, based on WTO figures.
a Weighted by China's imports of relevant items in 2000.
b At the end of the transition period.

the removal or reduction of subsidies. According to article 10 of the Protocol of Accession, China will eliminate all subsidies falling within the scope of article 3 of the Agreement on Subsidies and Countervailing Measures (SCM) of the WTO, namely "specific" subsidies paid upon export performance or those provided for domestically produced inputs in preference to imported products. For this purpose all subsidies provided to SOEs contingent on export performance will be viewed as "specific" if SOEs are the "predominant recipients of such subsidies" or if they receive "disproportionately large amounts of such subsidies". They would be regarded as specific since similar subsidies are not paid to private firms.[7] For agricultural production, domestic support of up to 8.5 per cent of output value is allowed, but all other subsidies, notably those contingent upon export performance, are not allowed. According to article 12 of the Protocol of Accession, "China shall not maintain or introduce any export subsidies on agricultural products". China has also agreed to comply with article 5 of the Agreement on Trade-related Investment Measures (TRIMs), and to eliminate foreign exchange balancing and local content requirements, as well as export or performance requirements.

3. State trading and non-discrimination

Following accession, China is subject to WTO rules on State-trading enterprises (Article XVII of the GATT) and on equal treatment of domestic and foreign firms and individuals (Article III of GATT 1994) within three years. The combination of these rules implies that, with few exceptions, all transactions by State-trading enterprises and SOEs should take place on a commercial basis; no favourable conditions can be accorded for the purchase or sale of inputs and outputs and in their pricing or procurement (including transactions on imports and exports). However, with regard to imports, State trading will continue to be permitted for five categories of agricultural products (grain, vegetable oils, sugar, tobacco and cotton), crude and processed petroleum, and chemical fertilizers. Similarly, a number of agricultural products (cotton, tea, rice, corn and soya bean), minerals and labour-intensive manufactured goods (including silk up to 2005, cotton yarn and some fabrics) can continue to be exported by State-trading enterprises (Protocol of Accession, Annexes 1A and 2A2).

China will also progressively extend the provision and scope of the right to trade for all firms, including foreign firms, and will aim at

---

[7] Social welfare charges paid to SOEs are also regarded as subsidies under the SCM Agreement.

offering full "national treatment" within three years (excluding the above-mentioned items, which can continue to be traded through State-trading enterprises). In other words, all foreign individuals and enterprises will be accorded the same treatment as domestic enterprises (article 5 of the Protocol). Article 5 also obliges China to discontinue, within three years, the practice of allowing a limited number of firms the right to trade within a restricted geographic region, referred to as "designated trading". A number of agricultural products (natural rubber, timber, plywood and wool) and acrylic and steel products are currently traded in this manner (Protocol of Accession, Annex 2B).

Finally, for many services, foreign investment will be progressively liberalized. For example, upon accession a share of foreign ownership in telecommunications of up to 25 per cent is allowed in certain cities, but this will be raised to 49 per cent within three years and extended to cover more cities. Within five years, all geographical restrictions will be abolished. There are similar commitments for liberalization in banking and insurance.

C. Industrial structure, trade and employment

The above changes associated with China's accession to the WTO can be expected to have important consequences for that country's trade prospects and economic performance and for those of its principal trading partners and competitors. The crucial factor will be how vigorously China's industries can respond to the new set of incentives and restrictions, particularly on how effectively its export sectors exploit the new opportunities presented. As indicated above, given the dualistic structure of its economy, the costs and benefits involved in accession will affect different sectors differently, with difficulties likely to be experienced mainly in sectors dominated by SOEs and in agriculture. The analysis that follows suggests that while the problems of adjustment that could be faced in import-competing sectors may be serious, they are not insurmountable; on the other hand, the nature of China's export industry and market access conditions for labour-intensive manufactures sets limits to the gains that it could reap from accession.

There have been attempts to simulate and predict the overall impact of accession on trade and economic activity in China by using the so-called "general equilibrium" approach, mostly through Global Trade Analysis Project (GTAP) models. According to these simulations, accession will not have an impact on the overall level of employment in China, but there will be intersectoral shifts in employment and output

(Gilbert and Wahl, 2000). As is the case in any trade liberalization, accession will expand trade relative to output. Nevertheless, there are contradictory results concerning the relative impact of accession on imports, exports and output, which appear to be due to differences in the models used. For example, according to a World Bank study for the year 2005, the impact on exports would be more pronounced than on imports (Ianchovichina, Martin and Fukase, 2000). In an earlier estimate by the International Monetary Fund (IMF), based on the assumption that China would enter the WTO in late 2000 or early 2001, the immediate impact on the current account would be positive, but it would turn increasingly negative over the period 2002–2004, before becoming significantly positive in 2005. It was suggested that any deterioration in the current account would be largely compensated by FDI inflows (IMF, 2000a: 63–65). The impact of accession on China's gross domestic product (GDP) would be negative, according to the World Bank study, but IMF estimates give a slightly positive effect for the period 2000–2005, except for the first year. An earlier study by the United States International Trade Commission (USITC) estimated that the Chinese offer for the bilateral agreement with the United States would increase Chinese imports and exports by 14.3 per cent and 12.2 per cent, respectively, thereby providing a significant growth stimulus for China (USITC, 1999).

The difficulty with such "general equilibrium" models is that they tend to assume away the problems which, in reality, determine the outcome. Particularly with regard to unemployment, it is generally assumed that the labour market remains in equilibrium (i.e. total employment will not change) but that labour shifts rapidly among sectors in response to new incentive structures. In reality, however, such shifts are extremely problematic, which is one of the reasons why many industrialized countries are unwilling to remove entry barriers to markets for labour-intensive manufactures and agricultural commodities (UNCTAD, 2001; *TDR 1995*, Part Two, chap. II). Moreover, accession to the WTO does not completely remove the danger of protectionism. Success in export drive can trigger defensive protectionist reactions in the form of safeguards and anti-dumping. Most of the models that are constructed on the principle of free markets do not allow for such factors.

A rigorous analysis of the implications of accession requires a good understanding not only of the conditions attached to accession, as noted above, but also of the structural and institutional characteristics of the sectors which will encounter new challenges due to the dismantling of support and protection, as well as of the potential for sectors that are better placed to exploit new trading opportunities that may arise from accession. This is the main focus of this section.

1. Trade liberalization, public enterprises and employment

China is entering the WTO while undertaking economic reforms – a process that has been under way for over two decades – in such areas as trade and industrial policies, labour market regulations, SOEs and social security. These efforts, particularly the reform of SOEs, which hold an important place in the Chinese economy, have no doubt helped to prepare the economy for accession. However, restructuring and rationalization in this sector is incomplete, and these enterprises are likely to face increased competitive pressures following China's accession. Accession is often seen as creating new opportunities and catalysing the reform process, but, unless properly managed, reforms can inflict social costs by leading to greater unemployment. Although China has experienced sustained and rapid growth over the past two decades, unemployment is relatively high.[8]

In spite of some shift in economic activities from the public to the private sector, SOEs still play an important role in the Chinese economy. These enterprises operate in a wide range of sectors including agriculture, industry and services: they are dominant in heavy industries such as power, steel, chemicals and armaments; and in banking, telecommunications, wholesale distribution and certain transport activities private firms are practically non-existent. However, in some light industries, such as toys, footwear and garments and retail consumer goods, private firms have a much higher share than SOEs. At the end of the 1990s, SOEs employed about 83 million people – representing 12 per cent of total employment and 47 per cent of employment in the manufacturing sector – and they accounted for 38 per cent of GDP (National Bureau of Statistics, 2000, tables 5–10). They account for about 45 per cent of China's imports and about 50 per cent of its exports, but these exports constitute a small proportion of their overall production: about 9 per cent of GDP in terms of gross value and a smaller proportion in value-added terms. Primary goods account for 15 per cent of their exports, and chemicals, textiles, light manufactures, rubber products and machinery and transport equipment for the remainder.

---

[8] For a discussion on the employment impacts of accession, see Bhalla and Qiu (2002), and Bhattasali and Masahiro (2001, appendix table 1) on the contribution of various sectors to growth in employment.

State-owned enterprises are characterized by excessive employment, high inventory levels, low productivity, low capacity utilization, inefficient scales of production and outdated technology. Despite several years of reform, many of these problems persist,[9] generally leading to losses; if they show surpluses (profits), these are negligible compared to their huge stocks of capital. Subsidies paid to SOEs have decreased in recent years, but the growing losses of industrial SOEs, as a proportion of their value added, have increasingly been financed by credits from the banking system.[10] Some SOEs, such as those in the automotive industry (box 3.1), also benefit from preferential treatment in obtaining loans and foreign currency contingent upon their export performance, as well as preferential tariffs subject to meeting targets for local content of finished goods.

Box 3.1

EFFECTS OF TRADE LIBERALIZATION ON THE AUTOMOTIVE INDUSTRY

The automotive industry, particularly automobiles, is an example of an inefficient, highly protected industry dominated by SOEs, which will be considerably affected by trade liberalization resulting from accession. There were more than 2,000 enterprises engaged in the industry in 1999, of which 120 were assemblers of cars and trucks (Powell, 2001: 47; Bhalla and Qiu, 2002). The industry as a whole employs 1.8 million workers. The share of value added in output and the share of profits in value added are low, and the sector exports only 2 per cent of its output. Automobiles benefited from 80–100 per cent nominal tariff rates in 1999, down from a range of 110–150 per cent in 1995–1999. The industry is subject to licensing quotas, and automobile imports, in particular, are also subject to non-tariff restrictions (USITC, 1999, tables 3–2 and E-1). Thus the share of imports in total sales was less than 7 per cent in 1999, falling from about 10 per cent in 1995 as a result of expansion of assembly operations in joint ventures with foreign companies.

---

[9] For instance, although Angang Iron and Steel Company has cut 30,000 jobs since 1995, its labour productivity is one sixth that of Posco of the Republic of Korea (Powell, 2001:51). For modernization and lay-offs, see Bhalla and Qiu (2002). Sometimes the laid-off workers remain on the payroll and continue to receive a partial salary for a specified period. There were about 5.6 million such workers in 1995, increasing to 16 million in 1998 (Yang and Tam, 1999).

[10] In 1997, losses of these enterprises amounted to 3.4 per cent of their value added, and less than half of this was financed by subsidies (Broadman, 2000). For profitability, see Choe and Yin (2000).

Collective enterprises, and particularly SOEs, dominate the sector, in terms of both employment and sales, although their share has declined in recent years: the number of workers employed by SOEs fell from 1.5 million in 1995 to about one million in 1999, while those employed by collective enterprises fell from 196,000 to 126,000 over the same period. Despite a sharp increase in private sector activities, total employment in the industry fell by 7 per cent. However, the decline in sales by public enterprises has been more than offset by increased sales by joint ventures, and particularly other private enterprises, which together increased their shares from 30.3 per cent in 1995 to 58.7 per cent in 1999.

The industry suffers from excess capacity, which reached 46 per cent in 1998. Labour productivity is also low and the unit labour cost is high. Only 2–4 vehicles are produced per worker a year compared to 20–40 vehicles in more advanced countries (Yang, 1999). An automobile made in China is 40–50 per cent more expensive than a similar make produced abroad.

For the motor vehicle industry there will be significant tariff reductions in the first two years following accession. In particular, tariffs for automobiles will fall from 80–100 per cent to 25 per cent by July 2006, with the largest cuts taking place soon after accession. Moreover, the ceiling for what is currently a prohibitive import quota will be raised to $6 billion upon accession and will increase further by 15 per cent per year until it is fully eliminated. All services related to automobiles will be liberalized: distribution, marketing, after-sale services, financing, dealership, advertising and imports of parts will be opened up to foreign firms. Other changes include the abolition of local content requirements, reduction of tariffs on parts and elimination of subsidies.

UNCTAD simulations suggest that, as a result of tariff reductions alone, output can be expected to decline by more than 11 per cent by the year 2005, and the ratio of imports of motor vehicle and parts to output to increase by 9 per cent (see table 3.2). More importantly, loss of employment of skilled and unskilled labour could reach about 12 per cent and over 8 per cent respectively, resulting in about 200,000 job losses in the sector. These figures do not take into account the adverse effects of the abolition of the local content requirement and preferential access to loans, and the elimination of subsidies.

Removal of subsidies, reduction of tariffs and NTMs, and elimination of preferential treatment will, no doubt, exert considerable pressure on these enterprises to improve efficiency and competitiveness, which may call for considerable restructuring and labour-shedding. Big bang liberalization can be both socially disruptive – particularly in the hinterland, where many SOEs are located – and economically counterproductive, as demonstrated by the experience of the Russian

Federation and Eastern Europe (ECE, 1997: 75–84; 1998: 31–41). The scale of restructuring that remains to be done is immense. It has been estimated that about 35 million workers, or 17 per cent of the urban work force, are redundant (JP Morgan, 1999: 14). According to a recent study (Powell, 2001), China's accession to the WTO could cause unemployment to rise as high as 25 million over the period 2001–2006.

The experience with trade liberalization in developing countries shows that a sudden dismantling of support to and protection of domestic industry can have serious repercussions on employment conditions, resulting in job losses and widening wage differentials (*TDR 1997*, Part Two, chap. IV; UNCTAD, 2001). It can also lead to deindustrialization, particularly in sectors confronted with competition from the mature industries of more advanced countries. Often, it is difficult to shift displaced labour to export sectors, particularly when skill-mix requirements are different and the prevailing productive capacity is inadequate. Adjustment to new sets of incentives is not instantaneous; rather, it is a time-consuming process requiring investment in physical and human capital. In addition, for a large country like China, there is the further risk of flooding the market in labour-intensive products, particularly if restrictions on market access in industrial countries persist.

The SOEs likely to be worst affected by accession operate in industries such as machinery, electrical equipment, smelting and processing of metals, textiles, chemicals and chemical fibres, transport equipment, non-metal mineral products and food processing. Together these industries account for 72.5 per cent of the workforce employed by SOEs (Bhalla and Qiu, 2002). The last column of table 3.2 gives the import/output ratios, in 1997, for the main agricultural and industrial sectors. For some manufacturing sectors imports are low compared to domestic production, in large part owing to the protection and support provided to them. While some industries, notably machinery and equipment, are not heavily protected and there are large amounts of imports of such products, they may, nevertheless, face some pressure due to liberalization during the period immediately following accession. Two sectors particularly vulnerable to liberalization and import competition are the automobile and textiles industries (boxes 3.1 and 3.2, respectively). In the case of textiles, exports and imports are both important. Even though the sector is highly protected, the SOEs involved incur losses. For minerals and metals, although the tariff rates are not high, the extent of tariff reductions will be significant.

Table 3.2

SIMULATION RESULTS FOR THE IMPACT OF POST-ACCESSION TARIFF REDUCTION ON OUTPUT, EMPLOYMENT AND IMPORT/OUTPUT RATIO IN CHINA, BY SECTOR, 1997–2005

	Difference between accession and non-accession[a]				
		Employment			*Memo item:*
	Output volume	*Unskilled labour*	*Skilled labour*	*Import/output ratio*	*Import/output ratio in 1997*
Sector of production		*(Per cent)*		*(Percentage points)*	*(Per cent)*
Oil seeds	-53.5	-60.6	-61.5	92.3	40.2
Beverages and tobacco products	-38.7	-35.3	-38.8	46.8	4.6
Vegetable oils and fats	-6.5	-4.5	-7.3	19.4	43.0
Motor vehicles and parts	-11.1	-8.1	-11.7	9.0	15.4
Other crops	-8.8	-12.1	-12.7	8.8	7.7
Textiles	2.1	3.7	0.6	6.7	22.0
Grains, vegetables, fruits	-4.8	-7.7	-8.3	4.9	1.7
Dairy products	-3.8	-1.9	-4.7	4.6	21.8
Machinery and misc. manufactures	-2.1	-0.2	-3.5	3.5	20.9
Wood products	-1.5	0.4	-2.8	2.8	16.9
Electronic equipment	14.4	15.5	12.5	2.7	59.5
Clothing	22.0	22.6	19.9	2.5	7.2
Mineral and metal products	-2.6	-0.5	-3.8	1.8	10.0
Forestry and fishing	-0.0	-0.0	-0.5	1.8	3.0
Processed rice	0.2	1.8	-0.9	1.2	1.1
Transport equipment	-1.5	0.5	-3.0	0.9	35.4
Fuels and minerals	-0.4	-1.5	-2.0	0.8	15.2
Chemical and petroleum products	0.5	2.4	-0.7	0.7	22.9
Services	1.8	3.9	0.4	0.0	3.2
Leather products	13.7	14.5	11.8	-0.0	11.2
Meat and meat products	5.4	6.7	4.1	-0.3	11.7
Animals and animal products	6.6	5.3	4.7	-1.7	1.7
Food products	6.0	7.3	4.8	-2.0	9.1

Source: UNCTAD secretariat calculations, based on simulation using a model developed by Global Trade Analysis Project (GTAP) (Hertel, 1997).
a The comparison is between the values resulting from the simulation of China's performance after its accession to WTO and the values for a hypothetical situation without China's accession.

Table 3.2 shows the results of simulations on the impact of tariff reductions alone on output and employment in various sectors, in terms of deviation from the baseline, as of 2005. These results are partial and are not intended to describe the overall impact of accession on various sectors or on the economy as a whole. They should be interpreted with considerable caution since they do not take into account a number of factors noted above, including the impact of NTM reductions, elimination of subsidies, selective dismantling of policies, difficulties in moving labour across sectors or problems of market access. This might lead to underestimating losses and overestimating gains. Nevertheless, simulations are useful in identifying the sectors that are vulnerable to liberalization and the order of magnitudes involved.

The results indicate a nuanced picture. The impact of China's accession to the WTO on output and employment could be positive for clothing, electrical equipment, leather products, animals and animal products, meat and miscellaneous food products; most other manufactures and agricultural products may be adversely affected. With a few exceptions, imports could rise relative to domestic production, and the increase could be particularly rapid in sectors such as beverages and tobacco products, most agricultural goods, motor vehicles, textiles and, to some extent, machinery. In textiles, the impact of the accession on domestic production could be negative even if, as suggested by the results of simulations, exports were to expand (box 3.2). In most cases, output losses are associated with the loss of unskilled, and particularly skilled, labour. Industries likely to be the most severely affected in terms of job losses are those dominated by SOEs, identified above. The shift in employment, from import-competing sectors to export sectors, needed to offset job losses could be significant, notwithstanding the problems of market access.

Box 3.2

TEXTILE AND CLOTHING INDUSTRIES IN CHINA:
THE IMPACT OF LIBERALIZATION

There are indications that accession to the WTO could have a significant impact on the textiles industry in China. Unlike clothing, this industry is characterized by obsolete machines, low productivity, low-quality products and excess labour (USITC, 1999, chap. 8). It employs 5.8 million persons, compared to 2.1 million in the clothing industry, and its total output is more than double that of the clothing industry. In 1999, the textiles industry accounted for about 6 per cent of China's industrial output and 14 per cent of the industrial workforce. It is dominated by loss-making SOEs and there are a large number of enterprises with low labour productivity. This is in contrast to the clothing industry, where SOEs are profitable and account for a small share of total sales. According to some estimates, in 1998 about 40 per cent of SOEs in the textiles industry were on the verge of bankruptcy (USITC, 1999: 8-8 and table B.3). In general, the industry produces relatively low quality products, using traditional, labour-intensive techniques, although recently new FFEs have established some plants with more advanced technology.

INDICATORS OF CHINA'S TEXTILES AND CLOTHING INDUSTRY,[a] 1999

	Textiles industry			Clothing industry		
	All enter-prises	SOEs	FFEs	All enter-prises	SOEs	FFEs
Number of enterprises	10 981	3 011	3 032	6 611	792	2 864
Sales (*billions of yuan*)	414.8	148.2	88.3	184.7	13.5	90.9
Percentage share in total sales of the industry	100.0	35.7	21.3	100.0	7.3	49.2
Value added as a percentage of output	24.7	26.9	24.2	24.8	28.4	24.9
Value added per worker (*yuan per year*)	21 900	15 300	38 500	24 500	16 800	25 800
Profits (*billions of yuan*)	3.90	-0.14	1.29	6.20	0.13	2.64
Profits as a percentage of sales	0.94	-0.09	1.46	3.36	0.96	2.90

Source: National Bureau of Statistics, *China Statistical Yearbook 2000.*
   a   Only enterprises with annual sales of 5 million yuan or more are considered.

The relatively high ratio of textile imports to domestic production (22 per cent) is not indicative of an absence of protection for domestic industry; rather, it signifies the dependence of clothing exports on imported textiles, particularly at the high end of the market: "about 55 per cent of China's exported apparel is made from imported fabrics" (USITC, 1999: 8-5). The expansion of clothing exports is the main reason why the ratio of textile imports to exports has risen sharply in recent years.

Recent reforms in the textiles industry have involved a shift of ownership, from SOEs to FFEs, mainly from Hong Kong (China); this has been accompanied by the introduction of more recent technologies, more capital-intensive methods of production and higher labour productivity. It is noteworthy that because of the recent introduction of new capital-intensive techniques by FFEs in the textiles industry, their labour productivity is now higher than that of the SOEs in this industry and also higher than that of FFEs in the clothing industry.

The reform of the textiles industry has also involved considerable labour shedding: while output barely changed during the period 1995-1999, employment declined by 35 per cent in the industry as a whole and by about 52 per cent in firms with sales of more than 5 million yuans. This was not compensated by higher employment in the clothing industry; on the contrary, while output in the clothing industry increased by 37 per cent between 1995 and 1999, employment declined by 23 per cent, in large part as a result of structural reforms and changes in ownership.

SOEs involved in the textiles industry have been running losses despite nominal tariff protection of the sector of more than 20 per cent. Their performance will further deteriorate as a result of significant reductions in tariffs and the reduction or removal of subsidies following accession. The liberalization of trade in clothing can also be expected to influence the competitiveness of the Chinese textiles industry. So far, low quality textiles produced by China have been used largely for the manufacture of clothing for domestic consumption, and imports of high quality clothing have been restricted by high tariff rates. Liberalization of clothing imports could shift domestic demand in favour of high quality clothing, which may lead to increased imports of high quality textiles. Although over time the quality of domestic textiles and clothing can be expected to improve, the short- to medium-term impact of accession could favour a rapid growth in imports of textiles. It is quite likely that the combination of accession and structural reforms could lead to even more labour shedding in the textiles industry, particularly since China will gain little additional market access in textiles and clothing in the short and medium term.

2. Foreign direct investment, employment and trade

It is generally expected that China's accession to the WTO will generate a surge in its exports. This has implications for other developing countries competing with China both in their own markets and, more importantly, in the markets of the major industrialized countries. Indeed, the simulations reported above suggest that the changed incentives structure resulting from trade liberalization could lead to a significant expansion of exports in a number of sectors, including electronics, apparel, leather products and other light industries. However, it appears that it is mainly improved market access, rather than the productive potential and competitiveness of China, that will determine export performance in most of these industries. If market access conditions for China do not improve following accession, changed incentives may not easily translate into rapidly rising export revenues.

These considerations apply largely to traditional labour-intensive manufactures. By contrast, trade could expand rapidly in sectors which are linked to international production networks. Indeed, one of the benefits expected from accession is increased inflows of FDI from both inside and outside the region. Liberalization of trade and investment as a result of the accession, notably relaxation of the restrictions on foreign participation in joint ventures and equal treatment of foreign and national companies, will provide foreign firms with greater investment opportunities. In fact there are already some indications of a rapid increase in FDI inflows into China: after hovering at around $40 billion during the period 1996–2000, they rose to $47 billion in 2001, at a time when they were declining in other parts of the developing world. According to some preliminary figures, in January 2002, FDI had increased by 33.5 per cent over the previous year, and contractual foreign investment, which tracks future projects, by 48 per cent (*International Herald Tribune*, 12 February 2002).

Some of this investment is motivated by the need for establishing a commercial presence for collaboration with certain domestic industries so far closed to foreign companies, notably in services; another important motive is likely to be the desire to take advantage of China's low labour and infrastructure costs. This tendency is reinforced by the pressure that the current global downturn is exerting on firms to maintain sales by cutting costs. According to a recent survey, one fifth of Japanese TNCs plan to relocate production to China (UNCTAD, 2002). For reasons discussed in the previous chapters, such a surge in FDI would result in increased two-way, or even three-way, trade in sectors that are involved in international production networks. Thus, expansion of FDI is expected to be associated with a rapid rise in exports and imports. Similarly, China's accession to the WTO may encourage firms to further outsource production to China of traditional labour-intensive manufactures, such as clothing, to take advantage of special tariff provisions in industrialized countries, notably the United States, for products that contain inputs originating from their home countries.

According to available data, the cumulative stock of FDI in China now amounts to over $350 billion, almost exclusively in greenfield projects. Most of this investment comes from the leading industrialized countries (Japan, the United States and members of the EU) as well as from the East Asian NIEs. However, a large number of FFEs are owned by investors of ethnic Chinese origin from Hong Kong (China) (about 48 per cent), Taiwan Province of China (8 per cent) and Singapore (about 6 per cent);[11] those from Japan, the United States and the EU each own 7–9 per cent, but their investments in China have been rising more rapidly in

---

[11] According to one estimate, 15–25 per cent of FDI inflows into China in the 1980s and early 1990s were round-trip investments originating in China. This is about half the inflow from Hong Kong (China) (Huang, 2002: 23).

recent years (JP Morgan, 2001: 69).[12] Much of the FDI originating from industrialized countries is oriented towards China's domestic markets, and an important share of the production and imports of the FFEs is for sale in China. For instance, it has been noted that:

> [While] US exports to China roughly tripled between 1990 and 1998, affiliate sales soared by more than 21 times over the same period (1998 is last year of available affiliate data). That is, from a low base, to be sure – affiliate sales in 1990 totalled just $639 million. Nevertheless, in 1998, US exports to China and affiliate sales were roughly equal at $14.2 billion and $13.9 billion, respectively. (Morgan Stanley, 2001)

The strong increase in income transfers and reinvested earnings by United States TNCs in more recent years, from $543 million in 1998 to $2 billion in 2000, suggests that this trend is continuing (Lowe, 2001). There are also some exports by United States affiliates in China back to the United States that benefit from special tariff provisions provided to imports containing inputs originating in their home country.[13]

Foreign-funded enterprises (FFEs) in China, owned mainly by investors from East Asia, are generally small and medium-sized enterprises (SMEs) that are highly export-oriented and involved in the last stages of processing and assembly operations. These FFEs have a higher degree of labour intensity and export orientation than those in the first-tier NIEs and the Association of South-East Asian Nations (ASEAN). Indeed, the share of their processed exports in total exports was over 55 per cent in 2000 (MOFTEC, 2001, table 4). The direct import content of exports by FFEs in China is high, estimated at some 50 per cent, and intra-firm trade accounts for as much as 30 per cent of imports of FFEs.[14] For FFEs involved in processing, the import content of their exports is even higher, at almost 70 per cent (MOFTEC, 1999). The ownership structure of these enterprises and the high import content of their manufactures have contributed significantly to strengthening the trade links between China and the East Asian economies, notably the first-tier NIEs and Japan.

---

[12] For the various features of FFEs in China, see Huang (2002: 23–32).
[13] Such imports rose tenfold between 1994 and 1998, reaching $2 billion in 1998 (Morgan Stanley, 2001).
[14] This is based on a survey undertaken by Long Quoqing in 2001 referred to in an UNCTAD discussion paper by Zheng (2002).

The share of FFEs in foreign trade has been rising rapidly in recent years: their exports increased from less than 2 per cent of total Chinese exports in 1986 to 48 per cent in 2000, while their imports rose from less than 6 per cent to almost 52 per cent. As noted above, SOEs account for much of the remaining exports and imports, while domestic private firms have a negligible share in foreign trade. Most FFEs are located in China's coastal and northern regions, where infrastructure is highly developed, and their activities are concentrated in the assembly of electronic equipment and in the production of machinery and equipment (Cerra and Dayal-Gulati, 1999; USITC, 1999, chap. I).

Since FFEs tend to use more capital-intensive techniques than local firms in similar industries, their contribution to job creation is modest, considering that their exports account for about 9 per cent of GDP; according to available data, these firms employed 5.4 million workers in 1996, or less than 0.8 per cent of the total labour force (Rosen, 1999: 87, table 3.1). This suggests that their scope for absorbing workers released from SOEs in labour-intensive export industries will be very limited.[15] Even if employment in export industries dominated by FFEs were to double, they cannot be expected to absorb more than a fraction of the labour expected to be released, according to even the most conservative estimates noted above.

Table 3.3 provides data on the origin of total merchandise imports and the destination of exports for China as a whole and for the FFE sector. A number of conclusions emerge. First, FFEs in China run a trade surplus primarily with the United States and deficits with the East and South-East Asian economies. This suggests that FDI from investors in East Asia uses China as an export platform for the Western markets, and that their home countries provide the inputs needed in such operations. Second, comparing the trade data for FFEs with total trade, it can be seen that China's export surplus is generated by national firms, notably SOEs, rather than foreign firms. Again, this is a reflection of the high import content of exports and low value added in the FFE sector.

---

[15] For a discussion, see Braunstein and Epstein (2002).

Table 3.3

REGIONAL COMPOSITION OF CHINA'S EXTERNAL TRADE, 2000

(Billions of dollars)

Trading partner	Total			of which: Foreign-funded enterprises		
	Exports	Imports	Balance	Exports	Imports	Balance
All economies	249.2	225.1	24.1	119.4	117.3	2.2
NIEs	66.6	63.2	3.4	36.0	39.2	-3.2
ASEAN[a]	11.6	17.1	-5.5	3.9	8.6	-4.7
Japan	41.7	41.5	0.1	23.3	28.4	-5.1
European Union	38.2	30.8	7.4	17.3	16.6	0.7
United States	52.2	22.4	29.8	28.8	10.0	18.8
Other economies	39.0	50.1	-11.1	10.1	14.5	-4.3

Source: UN/DESA, *Commodity Trade Statistics* database; Customs General Administration of the People's Republic of China, *China Customs Statistics Year Book 2001.*
a Excluding Singapore.

According to the latest available figures, total profits earned by FFEs in China were in the order of $20 billion (IMF, 2000b); this exceeded their export surplus by a wide margin. Thus they were in deficit in terms of foreign exchange earnings, which means that they had a negative impact on the current account. A significant proportion of their profits (about $12 billion) was reinvested in China, adding to the stock of FDI and, hence to the earning capacity of foreign firms (i.e. the foreign exchange deficit of the FFE sector was financed by new inflows of FDI). A similar situation was observed for Malaysia, as explained in *TDR 1999* (pp. 120–123). Meeting such deficits by simply relying on new FDI inflows would be similar to engaging in an unsustainable process of "Ponzi financing" (that is, servicing debt by incurring new debt).

Thus a surge in FDI runs the risk of resulting in a considerable expansion of both imports and exports without, however, bringing concomitant increases in value added and employment. This can be avoided if the nature and composition of the new investment were substantially different from the existing stock of foreign capital. This, in effect, appears to be the case with recent Japanese investment; there are signs that Japanese FDI in China may not simply involve relocating labour-intensive processes, but also the migration of a variety of large-scale industries, including capital- and skill-intensive ones, in chemicals and consumer electronics, for example. It has been suggested that "China appears to be 'leap-frogging' the development process seen in ASEAN countries, whereby Japan first invested in relatively 'low-tech' industries and only later in more 'high-tech' operations ... China is moving much more rapidly up the ladder" (*Oxford Analytica*, 2002). This second round of "hollowing out" by Japan, after the migration of some of its large-scale industries to South-East Asia in the early 1990s, is beginning to cause concern in that country, leading to pressures on China to revalue its currency in order to deter Japanese firms from shifting production to China (*TDR 1996*, Part Two, chap. I).

Certainly, the Chinese economy has the potential for developing self-contained, technology-intensive, large-scale manufactures that combine high quality human capital with low labour and infrastructure costs. It also has the market to support large-scale production. Such a process, based on rapid upgrading, can establish mutually reinforcing links between FDI, trade and growth. If such a route is not taken, and accession simply encourages the use of the Chinese economy as an assembly platform for low-value-added exports, the benefits of rising FDI inflows could be extremely limited in terms of technological upgrading and industrialization. This, together with the fact that China has not gained significant market access in traditional labour-intensive manufactures, implies that it may not realize the expected degree of benefits in terms of export expansion.

Again, the extent to which increased inward FDI creates competition for the developing economies in the region, notably the second-tier NIEs, depends on the nature of the investment. If it serves to relocate labour-intensive processes to China, such an approach may create trade-offs and stiff competition among countries with surplus labour and a high degree of reliance on FDI, and provoke a race to the bottom. In particular, competition for FDI between China and the less advanced developing economies of the region that have weak trade links with China can intensify, while China itself strengthens its trade relations with industrialized countries and the more advanced developing countries. Such problems can be avoided to the extent that FDI is used for technological upgrading and if greater attention is paid to domestic markets for absorbing the surplus labour.

D.   Trade prospects

The new trading opportunities for China will be mainly in labour-intensive manufactures and participation in the labour-intensive segments of the production process of high-tech manufactures. In these activities competition among developing countries will tend to increase. On the other hand, there will be an increase in China's imports of a number of capital- and technology-intensive products in sectors dominated by SOEs. Since the industrialized countries and the more advanced developing countries have a competitive edge in these products, they are likely to be the main beneficiaries of increased imports by China due to accession; other developing countries with export structures similar to China's, on the other hand, will probably face the greatest competitive pressure. Established trade links are important in both respects since, in the short run, it is easier to exploit existing links than to create new ones. The following section examines the sectors and products where such opportunities and pressures may develop, and how they affect various countries.

1.   Costs, competitiveness and market penetration

Low wages have been an important factor in China's impressive export performance, but they do not necessarily give the country a competitive edge in a wide range of manufactures because labour productivity is also low. China's average manufacturing wages are lower than those of the industrialized and developing economies listed in table 3.4, but its average manufacturing unit labour cost is higher than in seven of the developing economies. This is not surprising. Average labour productivity in China's manufacturing as a whole is low, despite the existence of highly efficient FFEs, because the SOEs suffer from excess labour and low productivity. Thus, as seen in that table, countries with much higher average manufacturing wages than China's (e.g. Chile, Mexico, the Republic of Korea and Turkey) have lower unit labour costs.

For labour-intensive manufactures, the picture should be different in view of China's export success in these sectors. However, comparative data on unit labour costs are not available at the sectoral level. Table 3.5 compares China's hourly labour costs, including non-wage labour costs, in textiles and clothing with those of a number of developed and developing economies. In developed countries, both textiles and clothing are more skill-intensive than in China, and figures on wages and labour costs are not directly comparable, as the quality of labour is different in

Table 3.4

WAGES AND UNIT LABOUR COSTS IN MANUFACTURING: COMPARISON BETWEEN CHINA AND SELECTED DEVELOPED AND DEVELOPING ECONOMIES,[a] 1998

Economy	Ratio to Chinese level of	
	Wages	Unit labour costs
United States	47.8	1.3
Sweden	35.6	1.8
Japan	29.9	1.2
Singapore	23.4	1.3
Taiwan Prov. of China (1997)	20.6	2.3
Republic of Korea	12.9	0.8
Chile	12.5	0.8
Mexico	7.8	0.7
Turkey	7.5	0.9
Malaysia	5.2	1.1
Philippines (1997)	4.1	0.7
Bolivia	3.7	0.6
Egypt	2.8	1.5
Kenya	2.6	2.0
Indonesia (1996)	2.2	0.9
Zimbabwe	2.2	1.2
India	1.5	1.4

Source: UNCTAD secretariat calculations, based on UNIDO, Industrial Statistics Database; and National Bureau of Statistics, *China Statistical Yearbook 1999*.

Note: Wages and unit labour costs include social changes and fringe benefits; for calculation of unit labour costs average wages were divided by manufacturing value added.

a   Ratios of average wages and unit labour costs in the economies listed to Chinese levels.

the two groups.[16] By contrast, the skill mix and labour productivity are unlikely to differ much among developing countries, particularly in clothing, where product standards are quite similar. As noted in box 3.2, labour productivity in Chinese clothing is much higher than in textiles. Consequently, lower Chinese labour costs are better indicators of its competitive edge in clothing, vis-à-vis other developing countries, than in textiles. The figures suggest that while China has a labour cost advantage in clothing compared to most middle-income economies, its competitive edge over India and Bangladesh, for example, is less clearcut.

---

[16]   In developed countries, the textiles industry is more capital-intensive, and thus requires more skills. Similarly, their clothing industry uses quality and designs that demand better skills and knowledge.

Table 3.5

HOURLY LABOUR COSTS IN THE TEXTILES AND CLOTHING INDUSTRIES: COMPARISON
BETWEEN SELECTED DEVELOPED AND DEVELOPING ECONOMIES AND CHINA,[a] 1998

Economy	Ratio to Chinese level of labour costs in textiles industry	Economy	Ratio to Chinese level of labour costs in clothing industry
Italy	25.5	United States	23.1
United States	20.9	Costa Rica	12.2
Taiwan Province of China	9.4	Hong Kong, China	12.1
Hong Kong (China)	9.1	Republic of Korea	6.3
Republic of Korea	5.9	Mexico	3.5
Turkey	4.0	Guatemala	3.0
India	1.0	India	0.9
		Bangladesh	0.7
		Indonesia	0.4
Memo item:			
Hourly labour costs in China			
(United States dollars)	0.62		0.43

Source: Based on USITC (1999), tables 8-2 and 8-4, which in turn are based on Werner International Management Consultants (1998).
    a Ratios of hourly labour costs in the economies listed to the Chinese level.

Differences in absolute costs and market access conditions, as well as non-price factors, are the most important determinants of the extent to which countries can penetrate international markets in different products. One way of measuring the combined impact of these factors is through the indicator known as revealed comparative advantage (RCA). This is defined as the share of a specific product in total exports of a country relative to the share of the same product in world trade. A ratio exceeding unity indicates that the country has a competitive advantage in that product. An increase in that indicator points to an improvement in the competitiveness of the country in that product. It should be noted that RCA is only a proxy, with some shortcomings. For example, since trade data are reported on gross value rather than on a value-added basis, the RCA indicator does not reveal where competitiveness lies for products with high import content, particularly those assembled in low-wage countries. This problem can partly be overcome by applying the indicator to imports as well as exports.

Table 3.6

**CHINA'S POSITION IN WORLD TRADE IN ITS MAIN
EXPORT PRODUCTS (AVERAGE, 1997-1998)**

SITC code	Product group	Product category[a]	China's total exports	World exports	RCA	ΔRCA
			Percentage share of product group in			
894	Toys and sporting goods	B	4.5	24.5	7.0	1.1
851	Footwear	B	4.4	23.0	6.6	1.0
845	Knitted outergarments	B	3.7	16.7	4.8	1.1
843	Women's textile outergarments	B	3.6	16.1	4.6	0.7
752	Computers	E	3.4	3.9	1.1	5.2
842	Men's textile outergarments	B	3.3	19.0	5.4	0.8
764	Telecom equipment, and parts	E	3.2	4.3	1.2	1.4
846	Knitted undergarments	B	2.7	17.3	4.9	1.1
893	Plastic articles	D	2.1	7.0	2.0	1.3
831	Travel goods	B	1.8	31.0	8.9	1.0
778	Electrical machinery	D	1.8	4.2	1.2	1.4
848	Apparel and clothing accessories	B	1.7	26.4	7.5	1.1
759	Parts of computers and office machines	E	1.6	2.8	0.8	1.8
899	Miscellaneous manufactures	F	1.6	16.4	4.7	0.9
775	Household equipment	D	1.6	8.8	2.5	1.3
652	Woven cotton fabrics	B	1.6	14.28	4.1	0.7
762	Radios	E	1.5	18.9	5.4	1.2
658	Made-up textile articles	B	1.5	18.6	5.3	0.7
821	Furniture and parts thereof	B	1.5	5.0	1.4	1.3
653	Woven man-made fibre fabrics	B	1.4	8.5	2.4	1.1
771	Electric power machinery	D	1.2	8.6	2.5	1.5
844	Textile undergarments	B	1.2	17.0	4.9	0.6
651	Textile yarn	B	1.2	6.5	1.9	0.9
776	Transistors and semiconductors	E	1.2	1.1	0.3	2.0
333	Crude petroleum	A	1.2	1.0	0.3	0.5
772	Electrical apparatus	D	1.2	2.9	0.8	1.4
699	Base metal manufactures	C	1.0	4.4	1.3	1.1
885	Watches and clocks	E	1.0	12.0	3.4	0.9
	Total shares of above items		57.7			

Source: UNCTAD database.
Note: RCA is revealed comparative advantage, which is used as an indicator for competitiveness. ΔRCA is the ratio of RCA for 1997-1998 to the RCA for 1992-1993.
   a The classification in this table of products into product categories follows that in Chapter 1 and *TDR 1996*, Part Two, chap. II. The categories are as follows: A = primary commodities; B = labour-intensive and resource-based manufactures; C = manufactures with low skill and technology intensity; D = manufactures with medium skill and technology intensity; E = manufactures with high skill and technology intensity; F = unclassified manufactured product.

Table 3.6 provides data on, and changes in, RCA for China's leading export products. The products in which China has a very high RCA are either from the traditional labour-intensive sectors (mostly in the SITC 8 product groups) or the technology-intensive sectors (mostly in the SITC 7 product groups), where China is involved mainly in the labour-intensive assembly operations. The labour-intensive products with high RCA account for more than 37 per cent of China's total exports, compared to 18 per cent for technology-intensive products. In some of the labour-intensive products, however, China is losing its competitive edge (notably outergarments, textiles and cotton fabrics), while the increase in RCA is particularly strong in sectors with high technology intensity. This includes a number of products in which China did not have a very high RCA to begin with, such as computers. Moreover, China has gained significant market shares in a number of other technology- and capital-intensive goods which account for less than 1 per cent of its exports, including ships and boats, rotating electric plants, trailers and non-motor vehicles, sound recorders, office machines and cement (Shafaeddin, 2002).

When the RCA indicator is applied to imports of components of a product, it reveals whether or not a country is competitive in assembly operations (Ng and Yeats, 1999). When it exceeds unity for a component, it suggests competitiveness in such operations. When applied to a finished product, the higher the RCA, the less competitive is the country in its production. While an increase in RCA for components implies that the country has become more competitive in assembly operations, for finished products a higher RCA implies that it is lagging behind more competitive producers.

Table 3.7 provides RCA values for China's leading imports. It includes both finished products and parts, which together account for nearly 63 per cent of China's total imports. Although some finished products also include imported parts, and hence there is some double counting, the number of such products is small; intermediate products and components constitute the bulk of the items in the table. As expected, most items in the table are products with high skill and technology intensity (SITC 7). Of the first 10 items with the highest RCA values, 7 are intermediate products and components, accounting for 27 per cent of China's imports. In fact, RCA values are high for all components and parts listed in the table, indicating that China is competitive in assembly operations. However, for some of these (telecommunications equipment and parts, rotating electric parts, non-electrical accessories of machinery, heating and cooling equipment and parts), RCA values show a decline

Table 3.7

**CHINA'S POSITION IN WORLD TRADE IN ITS MAIN
IMPORT PRODUCTS (AVERAGE, 1997-1998)**

| | | | | Percentage share of product group in | | | |
| | | | | China's | | | |
Rank	SITC code	Product group	Product category^a	total imports	World imports	RCA	ΔRCA
1	583	Polymerization products	E	5.5	9.8	3.8	1.3
2	776	Transistors and semiconductors	E	5.2	3.5	1.3	1.6
3	764	Telecom equipment, and parts	E	4.7	4.7	1.8	0.8
4	653	Woven man-made fibre fabrics	B	3.9	12.0	4.7	1.2
5	728	Specialized machinery and equipment	D	3.6	7.8	3.1	0.7
6	333	Crude petroleum	A	3.1	2.0	0.8	1.8
7	674	Iron or steel universals and plates	C	2.6	6.8	2.6	2.3
8	759	Parts of computers and office machines	E	2.6	3.1	1.2	2.3
9	792	Aircraft	E	2.3	3.8	1.5	1.1
10	334	Petroleum products	A	2.2	3.2	1.3	1.2
11	641	Paper and paperboard	B	2.2	4.2	1.6	1.7
12	651	Textile yarn	B	2.1	7.9	3.1	1.1
13	772	Electrical apparatus	D	2.0	3.8	1.5	1.6
14	562	Manufactured fertilizers	E	1.9	14.8	5.8	0.9
15	778	Electrical machinery	D	1.9	3.2	1.2	1.3
16	611	Leather	B	1.4	14.0	5.4	1.1
17	736	Machine tools for working metal	D	1.3	6.0	2.4	0.8
18	724	Textile machinery	D	1.3	8.0	3.1	0.5
19	874	Measuring and analysing instruments	E	1.3	2.8	1.1	0.97
20	686	Copper	A	1.3	5.7	2.2	0.9
21	716	Rotating electric plant and parts	D	1.2	5.6	2.2	0.9
22	652	Cotton fabrics	B	1.1	7.7	3.0	1.6
23	081	Feeding stuff for animals	A	1.1	6.5	2.5	3.2
24	749	Non-electrical accessories of machinery	D	1.1	2.4	0.9	1.0
25	281	Iron ore and concentrates	A	1.1	11.9	4.6	1.4
26	582	Condensation products	E	1.1	4.9	1.9	1.7
27	752	Computers	E	1.1	0.8	0.3	1.3
28	744	Mechanical handling equipment	D	1.0	4.0	1.6	1.2
29	741	Heating and cooling equipment	D	1.0	3.2	1.3	0.8
30	657	Special textile fabrics	B	1.0	7.4	2.9	0.9
		Total shares for above items		62.8			

Source: UNCTAD database.
Note: See table 3.6.
a See table 3.6.

between 1992-1993 and 1997-1998. This suggests that China has improved its capacity to produce such components. Finally, for some finished products (miscellaneous electrical machinery, measuring and checking instruments), their share in imports and their RCA indicators declined between 1992-1993 and 1997-1998, suggesting that the country is building up capacity in these sectors. These results are consistent with the findings of an earlier study, which concluded that China's capability in production and exports of components was greater than that of a number of ASEAN countries and NIEs, namely Hong Kong (China), Indonesia, Malaysia and Thailand (Ng and Yeats, 1999, tables 1 and A.1).

2. Competition with other developing countries

These changes in the composition and direction of China's exports and imports have important implications for other economies, although these will vary depending on their location in the international division of labour and on the technological scale. Competition would be greater with countries having a similar export structure to China's, while greater complementarity can be expected for countries which have the capacity to supply the products in which the Chinese economy does not have a competitive edge. In general, as noted above, the East Asian NIEs, and particularly some members of ASEAN, whose light manufactured goods account for the bulk of their exports, can expect to face greater competition from Chinese manufactured goods. In Latin America, Mexico is likely to face more competition from Chinese exports than other economies in view of the relatively higher share of manufactures in its exports. African countries are unlikely to be affected by greater competition since, with the exception of some North African countries and Mauritius, their manufactured exports are generally negligible.

Much of the competition in manufactured exports occurs in the markets of the major industrialized countries, notably the United States: it is the single most important market for Chinese capital goods. The EU is the leading market for China's chemicals, and the second for most other exports, while Japan is the largest importer of China's power-generating machinery. The United States is the main destination, followed by Japan and the EU in that order, for most Chinese light manufactures, except travel goods, articles of plastic, toys and sporting goods, for which the EU is the main market. For Chinese textiles and clothing exports, including exports channelled through Hong Kong (China), the United States is the main market.

China's penetration of markets of developing economies in manufactures varies in both extent and composition. It has closer trade links with the Asian economies, particularly the first-tier NIEs and ASEAN, than with the Latin American and African countries. However, less than 10 per cent of China's exports of light manufactures (mainly textiles and textile fibres, travel goods, clothing and leather products) go to Asian developing economies, and much less to other regions: about 2 per cent of light manufactures and 4 per cent of textiles go to Africa. A somewhat similar pattern is observed for Latin America, where clothing and travel goods are the leading imports from China. However, while these figures are small for China, they constitute an important share of the markets in smaller African and Latin American economies.

3.   China's imports from developing countries

As noted above, the opportunities for increasing exports to China as a result of its accession are likely to be strongest for countries at higher levels of industrialization as well as those rich in natural resources. Developed countries can be expected to benefit the most. Judging from its past trade linkages with China, the United States can benefit mainly from China's liberalization of agriculture and increased imports of some capital goods (mainly electrical machinery and components), while Japan and the EU countries can be expected to increase their exports of manufactured products, particularly textiles, electrical and non-electrical machinery, and motor vehicles.

Among the developing economies, the more advanced ones, such as the Republic of Korea, Singapore and Taiwan Province of China, as well as some of the ASEAN countries, are expected to increase their exports to China of manufactures, particularly capital goods which constitute a higher proportion of Chinese imports. Liberalization of China's agricultural imports can be expected to present new export opportunities not only for some Asian countries, which already have high shares in Chinese imports of such products (table 3.8), but also for some Latin American and African countries.

Table 3.8 shows that the bulk of Chinese imports of manufactures, food and agricultural raw materials comes from Asian developing economies. However, there are considerable intraregional variations in terms of their share in China's total imports. Although light manufactures and food are the main South Asian exports to China, their share in China's imports is about 1 per cent. By contrast, Taiwan Province of China, the Republic of Korea, Hong Kong (China) and Singapore are, in

Table 3.8

**SHARES OF SELECTED ECONOMIES AND REGIONS OF ORIGIN IN
CHINA'S IMPORTS, BY MAJOR PRODUCT GROUP, 1999**

(Percentage)

Items	United States	European Union	Japan	Hong Kong (China)	Asia[a]	Latin America	Africa
All products	11.8	14.8	20.5	4.1	34.4	1.8	1.3
Food, beverages and oils	21.3	10.8	4.2	1.0	19.4	17.8	1.3
Agricultural raw materials	12.1	8.6	6.8	1.0	34.6	4.9	5.1
Manufactured goods	12.2	16.8	23.7	4.9	33.1	0.4	0.2
Chemicals	14.6	10.0	18.7	2.7	42.4	0.4	0.5
Machinery and transport equipment	14.1	23.8	25.7	3.9	25.3	0.2	0.1
Other manufactures[b]	7.6	8.4	23.3	7.8	41.3	0.8	0.4

Source: UNCTAD secretariat calculations, based on UN/DESA, *Commodity Trade Statistics* database, SITC Rev. 2.
  a Excluding Hong Kong (China), Japan and West Asia.
  b SITC 6 and 8, less 68.

order of importance, the main sources of Chinese imports, and they are likely to benefit considerably from import liberalization by China. Trade conducted in the context of production sharing and outsourcing can only partially explain China's imports from these first-tier NIEs. Differences in the production and export structures of these economies account for much of the trade among them. While China has a competitive edge in labour-intensive manufactures, its capacity is limited in technology-intensive manufactures, including capital goods, in which some of the first-tier NIEs have made considerable advances. The Republic of Korea, in particular, is expected to benefit considerably from China's liberalization of the telecommunications and automobile sectors, through both trade and FDI; according to one estimate, that country's exports to China could increase by $1.7 billion a year (Cooper, 2000: 5).

The only significant manufactured products exported to China by Latin America are leather and leather products. Nevertheless, Latin America could benefit from China's liberalization of agriculture and consequent expansion of imports of agricultural products, particularly food. Currently, the only noticeable benefit possible for Africa is in agricultural raw materials. Expansion of Chinese imports of manufactures is unlikely to bring much benefit to countries in these regions in the foreseeable future in view of their limited supply capacity and ability to compete in such markets.

In a number of areas, expansion of China's exports of final manufactured products can be expected to be accompanied by a concomitant increase in imports because of the high import content of its exports. For example, as noted in box 3.2, China has been increasingly relying on imports of textiles for use in its clothing exports. The main suppliers of textiles to China are Taiwan Province of China (accounting for about 25 per cent of Chinese textile imports), the Republic of Korea and Japan (about 20 per cent each). In the past, the textiles industry was labour-intensive, but there has since been a shift to capital-intensive methods – mainly through robotization – in which the more advanced economies of the region have a competitive edge over China. In addition, the relocation to China of clothing plants from Japan, the Republic of Korea, Hong Kong (China) and Taiwan Province of China has contributed to China's imports of high quality textiles from these economies – a trend likely to increase with the expansion of China's clothing exports. Nevertheless, lesser developed countries in South and South-East Asia, which continue to use traditional labour-intensive methods in textile manufacturing and produce low quality textiles, are unlikely to benefit unless they rapidly upgrade their textiles industries.

Computers and office machines is another product category likely to be affected by China's accession. As seen in chapter 1, these items have been among the most dynamic products in world trade, and China has gained market shares in them partly through greater participation in production sharing in the region. An expansion of China's exports in this sector can be expected to result in a concomitant increase in imports of their parts and components until China fully exploits its own potential to produce them domestically. In the past few years, about 60 per cent of China's imports of components have originated from the East Asian NIEs and 27 per cent from Japan. Less than 30 per cent of China's finished products have been exported to the NIEs, 10 per cent to Japan and more than 60 per cent to the rest of world. Chinese imports of components are relatively evenly distributed between the less and more advanced NIEs: 18 per cent from Hong Kong (China) and Taiwan Province of China, 22 per cent from Singapore and the Republic of Korea, and 19 per cent from ASEAN (excluding Singapore). These strong regional trade links imply that while China competes with the NIEs in third markets for final products, at the same time it provides a considerable market for them in parts and components.

E. Conclusions: managing integration

China's accession to the WTO and its greater integration into the international trading system raise two sets of policy issues for that country. First, trading under a new set of rules and commitments will, no doubt, entail some adjustment problems over the short and medium term, notably loss of jobs and productive capacity in sectors dominated by SOEs. The key question in this respect concerns the kind of policy measures needed to ensure a smooth adjustment to new conditions. The second set of policy issues relates to trade and industrialization strategies. Here the key questions concern the extent to which China will rely on foreign markets and investment for industrialization and development, and the modalities of its participation in world trade. In other words, how does a carefully managed strategic integration, designed to accelerate industrialization and growth, differ from increased integration that relies on static comparative advantages driven by market forces?

Certain characteristics of the Chinese economy allow greater scope for managing rapid trade liberalization compared to most other developing countries. In middle-income countries a substantial reduction of tariff and quantitative restrictions on imports often releases pent-up demand for consumer goods, notably consumer durables such as cars and home appliances, leading to a surge in their imports. The greater the inequality in income distribution at the time of liberalization, the higher the demand for such products relative to the level of income. In China, however, despite rising wage differentials and income inequality, the demand for and growth of consumer imports can be expected to be limited. Furthermore, since Chinese industry is much less oriented towards the production of luxury goods, there is considerable scope for using domestic taxation – including excise and value-added taxes – and credit mechanisms to deter such imports. In this respect, the experience of the first-tier NIEs, notably the Republic of Korea, provides useful lessons (*TDR 1997*: 179–182).

The standard advice for countries that undertake rapid trade liberalization is to devalue in order to prevent a deterioration in their balance of payments. This is unlikely to happen in China in the near future; on the contrary, as noted above, the country is already under pressure to revalue its currency to deter relocation of industries from some of its more advanced neighbours. However, it is important that China retain its autonomy and option to use the exchange rate, if need be, to prevent serious disruptions in certain sectors of its economy. A judicious combination of currency adjustments and domestic taxes may help to absorb the shocks to vulnerable industries without causing serious distortions in resource allocation or violating the commitments that the country has made in its accession to the WTO.

China could invoke the provisions of Article XIX of the GATT and the Uruguay Round agreement on safeguards, which enable countries to take trade-restrictive actions to prevent serious injury to domestic industries, or threat thereof. Such safeguard actions should be combined with continued reform of the sectors concerned so as to ensure a smooth adjustment to new conditions arising from accession. The preceding analysis of the structure and competitiveness of Chinese industries has shown that serious injury may be caused in sectors in which the more – rather than the less – advanced trading partners of China have a competitive edge. Consequently, it can be expected that a full and transparent application of safeguard provisions, in compliance with the MFN obligation, will not cause serious impediments to the exports of most developing countries. Given its position in the global trading system, China is, in practice, better placed to utilize such provisions against disruptive trade originating from mature industries in its more advanced trading partners than from those in other developing country members of the WTO.

In the longer term, all these policies and reforms would need to be placed in the broader context of industrialization, growth and development in China. The analysis above shows that the scope for expanded, export-oriented activities to generate jobs and incomes for a large proportion of the labour force in China is limited. Furthermore, any large shift of the labour force to labour-intensive manufacturing runs the risk of flooding the markets and is likely to lead to increased protectionist barriers in the industrialized countries; this would have adverse consequences for other developing country exporters of such products as well as for China.

Various estimates and simulations clearly show the difficulties inherent in such a strategy. Even relatively modest shifts in the labour force to export-oriented, labour-intensive manufactures imply large increases in world supply of these products and in the share of China in world markets. For example, the simulation in table 3.2 implies that if the export sector were to compensate for the loss of employment in the import-competing activities due to tariff reductions alone, the ratio of exports of goods and services to GDP would need to reach 41.5 per cent in 2005 – a level highly unrealistic even for such a low-income country as China, given its size. In such a scenario, China's shares in world exports of clothing and leather products would be about 35 and 30 per cent, respectively. (For clothing, this implies that China would account for 70 per cent of the annual average growth of world exports.) Other estimates put these figures even higher. For example, the World Bank's estimate for the share in clothing is over 47 per cent, implying an annual growth rate of more than 37 per cent in China's exports of clothing (Ianchovichina, Martin and Fukase, 2000, tables 6 and 8). Another estimate puts China's share in world exports of clothing at 40 per cent for 2005 and 44 per cent for 2010 (Wang, 2000). It is unrealistic to expect that China's accession to the WTO will lead to such far-reaching changes in Chinese and world trade. Such an expansion of Chinese exports is not only likely to face structural barriers in China itself; it could also lead to intensified competition in labour-intensive manufactures, with attendant consequences for their prices and terms of trade.

On the other hand, any trade and industrialization strategy should recognize that China needs foreign exchange for financing imports associated with its continued rapid pace of capital accumulation, that – despite its large population – its economy may not yet be big enough to generate the demand needed to support some large-scale industries, and that competition in world markets is often essential to the success of late industrializers. Thus one might propose a rapid and well sequenced technological upgrading in manufacturing as an appropriate strategy which allows a shift from labour-intensive to technology- and skill-intensive manufactured exports. As noted above, a shift to high-value-added, supply-dynamic products would require a new strategy aimed at replacing imported parts and components with domestically produced ones. Such a strategy could also generate sufficient foreign exchange earnings without pushing the trade/GDP ratios to unsustainable levels. Moreover, it could help avoid the problem of a fallacy of composition and provide more space for less developed exporters of manufactures. Clearly, such a strategy would imply that for a large proportion of the labour force jobs would need to be created in domestic sectors, including services, while an important part of the skilled labour is transferred to export-oriented manufacturing. Over time, upgrading of skills would be essential for sustaining rapid industrialization.

In a sense, such a process appears to be already under way. As noted above, China continues to have a strong competitive edge in the assembly of skill- and technology-intensive products and processing for export, but it has also been improving its capacity to produce more complex parts, components and finished products. This process can be accelerated and combined with reforms designed to upgrade production in large-scale, capital-intensive manufacturing sectors dominated by SOEs. China appears to have the potential to do so: it has an abundant supply of educated labour, and the cost of such labour is extremely low compared to most other developing countries. The latest data available, for the mid-1990s, indicates that the number of university graduates in China exceeds a million, compared with about 380,000 for Indonesia and the Republic of Korea. Moreover, engineers and scientists account for 35 per cent of the graduates as against an average of 24 per cent for Indonesia, Pakistan, the Philippines and Thailand, and 48 per cent for Singapore and the Republic of Korea. Similarly, the number of technicians per million habitants is 200, which is less than for the Republic of Korea (318) and Singapore (301), but much more than for India (108), Malaysia (32) and Thailand (30) (UNESCO, 1999). Thus China has the potential to leapfrog the industrialization process rather than continuing to rely on absorbing the surplus labour in relatively low value-added, labour-intensive manufactures.

References

Agosin M and Tussie D, eds. (1993). *Trade and Growth – New Dilemmas in Trade Policy*. New York, St. Martin's Press.

Bhalla AS and Qiu S (2002). China's accession to WTO: Its impact on Chinese employment. UNCTAD Discussion Paper 163, November, Geneva.

Bhattasali D and Masahiro K (2001). Implications of China's accession to the World Trade Organization. Paper presented at DIJ-FRI International Conference, "Japan and China – Cooperation, Competition and Conflict" (sponsored by the German Institute for Japan Studies and the Fujitsu Research Institute), Tokyo, 18–19 January.

Braunstein E and Epstein G (2002). Bargaining power and foreign direct investment in China: Can 1.3 billion consumers tame the multinationals? Mimeo. Cambridge, MA, University of Massachusetts, Political Economy Research Institute.

Broadman HG (2000). *China's Membership in the WTO and Enterprise Reform: The Challenges for Accession and Beyond*. Washington, DC, World Bank.

Cerra V and Dayal-Gulati A (1999). China's trade flows: Changing price sensitivities and the reform process. Working Paper (WP/91/1). Washington, DC, International Monetary Fund, Asia and Pacific Department, and IMF Institute.

Choe C and Yin X (2000). Contract management responsibility and profit incentives in China's State-owned enterprises. *China Economic Review*, 11: 98–112.

Cooper C (2000). *The Impact of China's Accession to the World Trade Organization: Implications for Korea and Japan*. Seoul, Korean Economic Institute.

Customs General Administration (various issues). *China Customs Statistical Yearbook*. Beijing, People's Republic of China.

ECE (1997). The crisis in Bulgaria. *Economic Survey of Europe, 1996–1997*. Geneva, Economic Commission for Europe.

ECE (1998). The crisis in Russia. *Economic Survey of Europe, 1998*, no. 3. United Nations publication, sales no. E.98.II.E.25. Geneva, Economic Commission for Europe.

Ge W (2001). Financial sector restructuring and capital account management in China – Some lessons for economic integration. Mimeo. Geneva, UNCTAD.

Gilbert J and Wahl T (2000). Applied general equilibrium assessments of trade liberalization in China. Paper presented at the Workshop on China's Accession to the WTO on "An Overview of Recent Analyses", CPB Netherlands Bureau for Economic Policy Analysis and Institute of Qualitative and Technical Economics of the Chinese Academy of Social Science, Beijing, 19–20 October.

Hertel T, ed. (1997). *Global Trade Analysis – Modeling and Applications*. New York, Cambridge University Press.

Huang Y (2002). *Selling China: Foreign Direct Investment During the Reform Era*. New York, Cambridge University Press.

Ianchovichina E and Martin W (2001). *Trade Liberalization in China's Accession to the WTO*. Washington, DC, World Bank, 3 May.

Ianchovichina E, Martin W and Fukase E (2000). Assessing the implications of merchandise trade liberalization in China's accession to WTO. Paper presented to the Roundtable on China's Accession to the WTO sponsored by the Chinese Economic Society and the World Bank, 8 July, Pundong, Shanghai. Washington, DC, World Bank, 23 June.

IMF (2000a). *World Economic Outlook*. Washington, DC, International Monetary Fund.

IMF (2000b). *Balance of Payments Statistics Yearbook*. Washington, DC, International Monetary Fund.

JP Morgan (1999). China's reforms to take another costly decade. *Global Data Watch*. Hong Kong, 29 October: 9–29.

JP Morgan (2001). *Global Data Watch*. Hong Kong, 4 May.

Lowe JH (2001). *Survey of Current Business. U.S. Direct Investment Abroad*. Washington, DC, United States Department of Commerce, Bureau of Economic Analysis, September (www.bea.doc.gov/bea/pub/0901cont.htm).

MOFTEC (1999). Statistical data (on FDI). Beijing, Ministry of Foreign Trade and Economic Cooperation (www.MOFTEC.gov.cn).

MOFTEC (2001). *Report on the Foreign Trade Situation of China*. Beijing, Ministry of Foreign Trade and Economic Cooperation, Spring.

Morgan Stanley (2001). The latest views of Morgan Stanley Economists, 2 April. New York, Morgan Stanley Global Economic Forum (www.morganstanley.com).

National Bureau of Statistics (2000). *China Statistical Yearbook 2000*. Beijing, People's Republic of China.

Ng F and Yeats A (1999). Production sharing in East Asia: Who does what for whom and why? Policy Research Working Paper, 2197, Washington, DC, World Bank, October.

Oxford Analytica (2002). Tokyo vexed by flight of manufacturing. Daily Brief, 12 February (www.oxweb.com/default.asp).

Powell B (2001). China's great step forward. *Fortune*, September: 42–54.

Rosen DH (1999). *Behind the Open Door: Foreign Enterprises in the Chinese Marketplace*. Washington, DC, Institute for International Economics.

Shafaeddin SM (2002). The impact of China's accession to WTO on the exports of developing countries. UNCTAD Discussion Paper, 160. Geneva, June.

UNCTAD (2001). Globalization and the labour market. Paper prepared for the meeting of the ILO Working Party on the Social Dimension of Globalization, Geneva, 12 November.

UNCTAD (2002). FDI downturn in 2001 touches almost all regions. Press Release (TAD/INF/PR36). Geneva, 21 January.

UNESCO (1999) *UNESCO Statistical Yearbook*. Paris, United Nations Educational, Scientific and Cultural Organization (www.uis.unesco.org/uisen/stats/stats0.htm).

USITC (1999). *Assessment of Economic Effects on the United States of China's Accession to WTO*. Investigation no. 332–403. Washington, DC, United States International Trade Commission, September.

Wang Z (2000). *The Impact of China's WTO Accession on the World Economy*. Washington, DC, Economic Research Services, United States Department of Agriculture.

Werner International Management Consultants (1998). *Hourly Labour Costs in the Textiles Industry and Hourly Labour Costs in the Apparel Industry*. New York.

Yang M and Tam CH (1999). Xiagang: The Chinese way of reducing labour redundancy and reforming State-owned enterprises. *East Asia Institute (EAI) Background Brief*, 38. Singapore, 20 July.

Yang Y (1999). Completing the WTO accession negotiations: Issues and challenges. *World Economy*, 22: 513–34.

Zheng Z (2002). China's terms of trade in manufactures, 1993–2000. UNCTAD Discussion Paper No. 161. June. Geneva.